2nd Edition

INTRODUCTION
TO TWO-PART
SPECIES
COUNTERPOINT
A Summary of Fundamentals

Howard Cinnamon, Ph.D.

Professor of Music
Coordinator of Music Theory/Composition
Hofstra University

Linus
Publications, Inc.

Published by Linus Publications Inc.
Ronkonkoma, NY 11779

ISBN 10: 1-60797-387-1

ISBN 15: 978-1-60797-387-4

Printed in the United States of America.

This book is printed on acid-free paper.

Print Number   5   4   3   2   1

PREFACE

Between the early part of the eighteenth century and the beginning of the twentieth century, the pedagogical method for the teaching of principles of counterpoint know as Species Counterpoint played a central role in the basic training of virtually all musicians. Most of the great composers of the common-practice period, Haydn, Mozart, Beethoven, Chopin, Rossini, Liszt, Mendelssohn, Brahms, and many others, were trained according to this methodology, a fact that is born out by the almost universal incorporation of its principles into the musical style of the common-practice period. These concepts, therefore, represent more than a mere pedagogical methodology, they are the fundamental concepts of musical structure, the common practices (if you will) that identify and unify the common-practice period and still strongly influence musical composition, even today.

The species approach to counterpoint was first codified by J. J. Fux in his *Gradus ad Parnassum* (1725). He organized his method into five progressive species, which lead gradually from the simple to the more complex, increasing in rhythmic complexity and in the use (and control) of dissonances as they progress. The great strength of this approach lies in its goal of developing, within the student, the ability to recognize and control the essentials of melodic writing and voice leading without the distractions (or complications) associated with the preoccupation with "harmony" that often characterizes texts on counterpoint. This approach conditions students to consider counterpoint as an essential element of musical structure, even in music that is often considered "homophonic" and best prepares them for a sophisticated understanding of the contrapuntal derivation of harmonic relationships and of the fundamentally contrapuntal roles of many harmonies.

The study of Species Counterpoint should be carefully distinguished from that of Sixteenth-Century Counterpoint with which it is often confused. Sixteenth-Century Counterpoint is, by definition, a style study wherein the student is expected to emulate the compositional practices of a particular period (or composer) of the late sixteenth century. As such, its principles include many idiosyncratic and stylistically distinct practices that are not typical of the music of other styles and style periods.

Species Counterpoint, on the other hand, is an astylistic abstraction. It instructs in principles of musical structure that are common to all styles and style periods between roughly 1500 and 1900, including the sixteenth century, and offers a consistently applicable catalogue of general practices through which music of various styles may be compared and differentiated. When we understand and recognize the general principles employed in all styles, we can better identify and define the characteristic style of a given piece, composer, or period and recognize it as the individualized application of these general principles distinct to that piece, composer, or period. As such Species Counterpoint and the analytical methodology based upon it represent an invaluable tool for musicologists, music theorists, composers, performers, and all other musicians interested in better understanding individual pieces specifically, and western music in general.

Species Counterpoint also provides a system of clear guidelines for the students' first attempts at musical composition, allowing for strict pedagogical control over the materials and methods they can use, and helping them to gain gradual control over the basic elements of musical structure it is designed to teach. Because it is usually equally unfamiliar to all students, those with little or no previous training in theory can develop a clear understanding of basic principles before attempting to master more complex concepts, while those with a some previous background in theory can learn to overcome and discard any misconceptions or distortions that may have crept into their previous training.

As the title of this text indicates, this is a summary of these principles, designed for use as a basic reference text for the study of species counterpoint included in an introductory music theory class. It is by no means complete (for one thing, three-voice counterpoint is not even mentioned, let alone thoroughly discussed). It, rather, presents only the main points, the essentials that are necessary as preparation for the study of Harmony and Voice Leading to be taken up in succeeding courses. The more thorough study of strict counterpoint in two and three parts must, regrettably, be left for more advanced study.

The text that follows is based largely on two sources, both of which are twentieth-century landmark treatises on the role of counterpoint in musical structure: Felix Salzer, *Structural Hearing* (New York: Charles Boni, 1952; 2nd ed., New York: Dover, 1962) and Felix Salzer and Carl Schachter, *Counterpoint in Composition* (New York: McGraw-Hill, 1969). Both of these treatises are based largely on the work of Heinrich Schenker (1868-1935), particularly his *Kontrapunkt*, Books 1 and 2, Vol. II of his *Neue musikalische Theorien und Phantasien* (Vienna: Universal Editions, 1910 and 1922). This work is now available in a translation by John Rothgeb and Jurgen Thym, *Counterpoint Books I and II*, (New York: Schirmer Books, 1987). The student is encouraged to examine these sources with an eye for further study and for the perspective they offer on the analytical power of the approach to musical structure they represent.

TABLE OF CONTENTS

– Unit One –

Species Counterpoint: Basic Principles

Counterpoint: the art of writing one melody against another. The study of counterpoint is the study of voice leading (the coordinated motion of two or more melodic lines). We study Strict Counterpoint, an abstract representation of the principles that govern the freer counterpoint found in most pieces, so that we can better understand, hear, control, and recognize the fundamental relationships that arise when two or more melodic lines combine into a coherent unit.

Species Counterpoint: the study of strict (abstract) counterpoint in a progressive manner leading from the simplest to the most complex. The study normally progresses through five species, differentiated on the basis of rhythmic (and associated melodic and voice-leading) complexities: First Species, note against note; Second Species, two notes against one; Third Species, three or four notes against one; Fourth Species, syncopations (essentially note against note with rhythmic displacement); Fifth Species, florid counterpoint, a combination of the four previous species.

This text involves species counterpoint from a primarily compositional perspective, i.e., practice in writing counterpoint to a given melody, *cantus firmus* (CF), in each of several species.

Basic Principles of Counterpoint

Principles of Melodic Construction:
Simplicity should be a primary goal. The melodies to which you will be writing counterpoint are rather simple in their melodic construction. Your counterpoint should be equally simple, within the constraints of the assignment.

Species counterpoint is based on a vocal model. *Singability*, therefore, is an important consideration in matters of range, leaps, etc. In general, smaller melodic intervals are easier to sing than larger ones; therefore, your melodies should contain predominantly smaller intervals.

1) **Melodic Intervals**: Melodic intervals of an octave or larger, all dissonant leaps (sevenths and all augmented and diminished intervals), and all chromatic half-steps (e.g., C-C#, D-Db, etc.) are forbidden.

Permissible melodic intervals are:
major and minor seconds, major and minor thirds, perfect fourths, perfect fifths, and major and minor sixths.

2) **Direction**: Melodies should have clearly defined beginnings and goals. Good melodies will generally contain a clear climax or arrival point (usually a high point in melodies written above a *cantus firmus* or a low point in melodies written below). This will serve as the goal for melodic motion up to that point and for the starting point of motion to the cadence.

3) **Continuity**: Melodies containing many leaps tend to sound disjointed and lack continuity. For the sake of continuity, therefore, **melodies should move predominantly by step.**

4) **Variety**: Melodies that are too consistent lack interest. Interest may be obtained through changes in direction and through the selective use of leaps.

   Melodies should not consist of a straight line in a single direction (though clear, long range goals are desirable) and may contain some carefully handled leaps.

   Leaps should be used sparingly. **Any leap larger than a third should be followed by a change in direction.** In most cases the change in direction **should be by step.**

   Above all, the primary consideration should be *MUSICALITY*. Your subjective judgment as a musician must temper all other considerations.

Principles of Harmonic: (Vertical) Construction:

1) **Consonance and Dissonance**: While consonance and dissonance are relative, strict counterpoint considers them absolute for our purposes. Consonant intervals may be used freely (within certain limitations), but the use of dissonant intervals is tightly controlled (and even forbidden in some species).

   Consonances: *Perfect*: perf. unison, perf. fifth, perf. octave (and their compounds).
   Imperfect: major and minor thirds (tenths) and sixths.

   Dissonances: All seconds, sevenths, perf. fourths, (and their compounds), and all augmented and diminished intervals.

2) **Relative Motion**: Two simultaneous melodies may move, in relation to one another, in four ways:
   a) *Parallel Motion*: Voices proceed in the same direction and maintain a virtually constant distance (for this purpose, major and minor intervals of the same numerical value are considered equivalent).
   b) *Similar Motion*: Voices move in the same direction but do not maintain a constant distance.
   c) *Oblique Motion*: One voice moves while the other remains stationary.
   d) *Contrary Motion*: Voices move in opposite directions.

In general, this listing presents these types of motion from least desirable to most desirable (parallel being least desirable, contrary being most desirable). For variety's sake, however, a mixture of various types of relative motion is usually most effective.

3) **Forbidden Parallels**: Parallel perfect unisons, octaves, and fifths (and their compounds) (exx. e, f, and g) tend to destroy the independence of the voices (by doubling the same pitches) or too strongly suggest vertical stability (in the form of a fifth), thereby inhibiting forward motion; they are, therefore, forbidden. Parallel thirds, tenths, or sixths (ex. h), however, are permitted but should be used sparingly so as not to become monotonous (usually not more than three in succession).

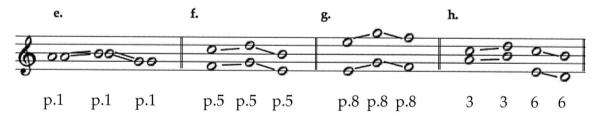

4) **Other Restrictions Involving Perfect Consonances:**
   Perfect Consonances approached in Similar Motion (ex. i) can be disruptive to the forward flow of the lines. This is due to our tendency to mentally fill in the skip that is present in the upper voice, producing a forbidden parallelism (ex. j). In two part texture like that we will be employing, this voice leading is to be avoided unless the upper voice moves by step (ex. k).[1]

---

[1] This exception derives from the 17th-century practice of Monody, in which the upper voice represented a solo part that might contain improvised embellishment while the lower voice represented the accompaniment, which was less likely to contain embellishment, hence, less likely to produce forbidden parallels.

Successive equivalent Perfect Consonances can be produced by contrary motion through the use of a compound interval (ex. l). Since the sound of this pattern strongly resembles that of parallel perfect intervals and also weakens the independence of the voices, this voice leading is to be avoided as well. Successions of different perfect consonances (e.g., 5-8-5, 8-5-8 or 1-5-8) can be very effective and should be employed freely.

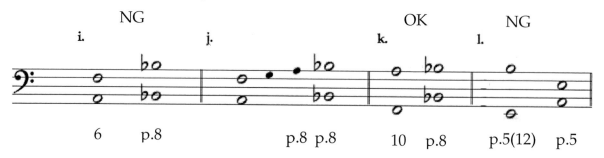

5) Other Restrictions on Voice Leading:

Simultaneous Leaps: Skips in both voices at the same time can destroy the coherence of the lines and of the counterpoint. This is particularly problematic with skips in similar motion and with skips larger than a fourth (ex. m). In general, avoid simultaneous skips, especially those in the same direction and those larger than a fourth.

Overlapping of Parts: If the lower voice moves to a tone above the preceding tone of the **upper** voice, or the **upper** voice moves to a tone **lower** than the preceding tone of the lower voice, this is said to be voice overlapping (ex. n). This makes it difficult to follow the motion of each voice individually and should be avoided.

Voice Crossing: The temporary shifting of the lower part above the upper part or the upper part below the lower part (ex. o), while an effective compositional technique in many styles, is inappropriate in species exercises and should be avoided. The relative position of the two parts should remain constant throughout each exercise.

Spacing: Because too large a distance between the voices can sound hollow and bare, the relative positions of the voices should remain within an octave. On occasion, for musical reasons, wider spacing maybe effective, but the distance between the voices should rarely exceed a tenth without very good reason, and never exceed a twelfth.

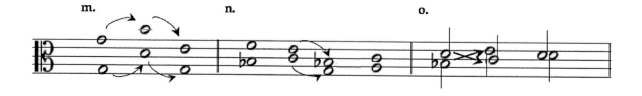

6) **B**eginning and Ending The Exercise: The most stable points in any counterpoint exercise must be the first and last verticalities. For this reason, only perfect consonances may be employed as the first or last vertical intervals in any exercise. But not every perfect consonance is equally acceptable in every circumstance.

At the beginning of an exercise, it is important to clearly identify the tonic immediately, so a verticality that does this clearly must be used. *When composing a melody above* a given CF, *this interval may be either an octave or a fifth* (unisons usually pose problems with voice leading, but would, theoretically at least, be acceptable if the voice leading could be made to work). *When composing a melody below*, however, a perfect fifth would suggest a different tonic (since we tend to here the lower pitch of the fifth as the most stable, i.e., tonic tone), thus *the most desirable intervals are an octave or a unison.*

At the end of an exercise, it is most important to produce a clear and stable cadence, *so the tonic must appear in both voices*, the *cantus firmus* and the counterpoint, forming either an octave or a unison. *In addition, the final tonic pitch must be approached by step and in contrary motion*, with the leading tone in one voice and scale-degree 2 in the other. The CF will always provide one; your counterpoint must provide the other. (In exercises in minor where the leading tone is approached by step from below, it will be necessary to raise scale-degree 6 as well as scale-degree 7 in order to avoid a melodically dissonant augmented second.)

7) **Notation of Counterpoint Exercises**: The *cantus firmus* and the counterpoint should appear on separate staves with bar lines running through from the top staff to the bottom. This kind of two-staff unit is called *a system* and represents one line of music. In many instances spacing needs will make it necessary to notate a melody in a register where a bass or treble staff would require numerous ledger lines. To avoid this notational problem and make your counterpoint more easily read it will often be advisable to employ an alto clef for one of the voices. In some cases, the *cantus firmus* will be given in alto clef. In most cases, however, the choice of clef for the counterpoint is optional any selection that represents the counterpoint effective and clearly may be chosen.

In addition to correctly notating each line of the counterpoint, each assignment should contain a rudimentary form of harmonic analysis. Each vertical interval formed between the two lines should be indicated below the lower staff according to their general names (e.g., 3, 5, 6, 8, 10). This will help you to avoid many voice-leading problems and will demonstrate that you understand and recognize correct voice-leading procedures.

Finally!!: Before doing each counterpoint exercise, reread carefully the following "Procedures of Writing," and keep them in mind as you work.

Exercises in species counterpoint offer effective training in both written and aural (ear training) skills. The ability to hear contrapuntal relationships, in particular, will be enhanced if these procedures are followed:

1) Sing the *cantus firmus* through several times before setting it. Study its shape with respect to high points and skips.
2) Never start work at the piano. Try to hear (mentally) what you write as you work; test the melodic quality of your counterpoint by *singing it*. After you have finished, test your exercise by singing one part and playing the other. Only when you have completed your work should you test your results by playing both parts on the piano.
3) Think in terms of *horizontal* continuity. Always plan three or four measures ahead as you work. Soon you will be able to workout an entire exercise mentally, before writing it. Try to work toward this goal.
4) After writing the exercise, *but before playing it on the piano*, check it over carefully for errors. Be particularly wary of melodic and harmonic diminished fifths and melodic augmented fourths, which look like their perfect counterparts. If you find too many of these, you are working too mechanically and not hearing what you are writing.
5) If you find an error, correct it carefully. It is quite easy to replace one mistake with another. It will often be necessary to rewrite several measures (or even the entire exercise) in order to correct what appears to be a minor problem. *Remember* above all, you are to make *musical judgments*. This may involve choosing the lesser of several evils, if a solution that has no problems cannot be found. Keep in mind, that, while some principles are inviolable (like forbidden parallels and rules of dissonance treatment), others are based on subjective judgments that may be overlooked if context justifies it.
6) In order to develop the capacity for planning ahead and mentally hearing a large part of the exercise, it is advisable to start by sketching the beginning, the close (cadence), and the general shape of the melody before filling in the details. While you may find it necessary to make changes in your plan as you work, having these guides will help organize your thoughts and insure the coherence of your finished work.

– Unit Two –

Two-Part Counterpoint: First Species

Rhythmic Organization:
Note-Against-Note (1:1)

Meter: $\frac{2}{2}$ (¢)

Durational Values: each tone of both *cantus firmus* (CF) and counterpoint equal a whole note (one measure).

Harmonic Material Available in this Species:
Consonant Intervals: p.1, p.5 (12), p.8, M.3 (10), m.3 (10), M.6, and m.6.
Dissonant Intervals: None in this species.

Melodic Restrictions:
In minor, the leading tone should be reserved for the cadence and should occur only immediately preceding the tonic. Elsewhere in the phrase, scale-degree 7 from the natural minor scale should be employed exclusively in order to avoid too strong a cadential feeling in mid-phrase.

Harmonic/Melodic Restrictions:
Avoid appearances of the chromatically altered leading tone too close to appearances of the unaltered scale-degree 7 (ex. a). When these two chromatic variants of the same scale degree occur in direct succession they produce either a *direct chromaticism* (ex. b), when they both occur in the same voice (forbidden as are all chromatic half-steps), or a *cross-relation* (ex. c), when they occur in different voices. Both are forbidden in all species.

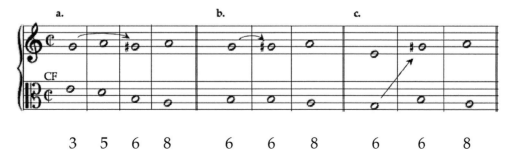

Harmonic Restrictions:

Phrase Beginning (1st interval): a perfect consonance (1, 5, or 8 with counterpoint above, 1 or 8 only with counterpoint below).

Mid-Phrase Restriction: no p.1 (unisons), which can destroy all sense of independent voices.

Phrase Ending (last interval), p.1, or p.8.

Below are a number of melodies, which may be used as *cantus firmi* in this species and in later ones. Those given with two key signatures and accidentals in parentheses may be used in either major or minor; the others may be used only the modes in which they are given. All may be transposed to other keys if desired. In some cases two additional cadence measures (in brackets) are given but are optional.

– Unit Three –

Two-Part Counterpoint: Second Species

All general principles of melodic and contrapuntal writing discussed to this point still apply. This species differs from first species only in these particulars:

Rhythmic Organization:

Two Notes-Against-One (2:1)
Two notes in the counterpoint to one in the *cantus firmus.*

Meter: $\frac{2}{2}$ (¢)

Durational Values (general character): each tone of *cantus firmus* equals a whole note, each tone of counterpoint equals a half note.
Metric organization: simple duple meter, resulting in accented and unaccented tones in the counterpoint.

Harmonic Materials Available in this Species:

Consonant Intervals: p.1, p.5 (12), p.8, M.3 (10), m.3 (10), M.6, and m.6.
Dissonant Intervals: p.4 (11), A.4, d.5, M.7, m.7, M.2 (9), m.2 (9).
         available only as passing tones (see below).

New Harmonic/Melodic Possibilities:

Basic Definitions:
Passing tone (P): A melodic embellishment in which a relatively unstable tone connects two *different* relatively more stable tones by step. The normal metrical position of a passing tone is weak compared to those of the more stable tones it connects. Passing tones may be either consonant or dissonant. This is the only context in which the dissonances listed above may occur in this species (see ex. a).

Neighbor Tone (N): A melodic embellishment in which a relatively unstable tone decorates two occurrences of the same relatively more stable tone by moving away from it by step and then returning to it. A neighbor tone may occur either above (upper neighbor) or below (lower neighbor) the primary tone. In second species, *only consonant neighbor tones may be used* (see ex. b)

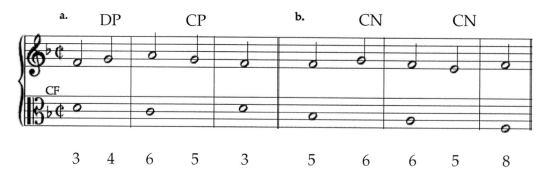

The first interval of each measure must be consonant; the second may be either consonant or dissonant. Dissonant tones must be approached and left by step, as passing tones. Consonant tones may be approached either by step or by skip.

Basic Roles of Second Half Note:

I.) *Fill in skips.*
  A) Dissonant or consonant passing tones (see above).
  B) Divide a large skip into two smaller intervals:
    1) a fifth or sixth may be divided into two smaller skips (ex. c) or
    2) a fourth may be divided into a step plus a skip or a skip plus a step, forming a "skipped passing tone" (exx. d and e).
       In both cases, the second half note must be consonant with the CF, and the large interval that is divided must be a consonant interval.
  C) Produce a consonant neighbor tone. To do so, the counterpoint must form a fifth followed by a sixth or a sixth followed by a fifth against the CF, since these are the only two consonances that can be formed by step-wise oblique motion against a sustained tone (see ex. b above).

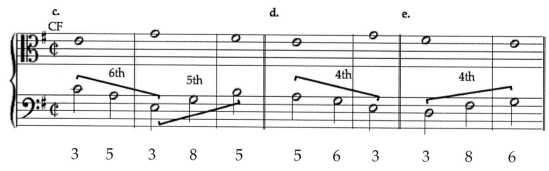

II.) *Provide melodic interest.*
  A) Change register through a skip followed by step-wise motion in the opposite direction (ex. f).
  B) Motivate a change in direction with a skip that requires step-wise motion in the opposite direction (ex. g).
  C) Substitute for a repeated note with another note that forms a consonance with the CF (ex. h).

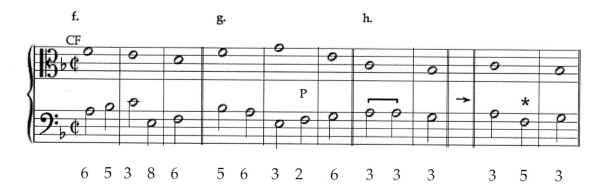

6 5 3 8 6   5 6 3 2   6   3 3   3   3 5 3

III.) *Avoid voice-leading problems* (especially parallel or similar 5ths and octaves) by substituting a skip for a step (exx. i-j).

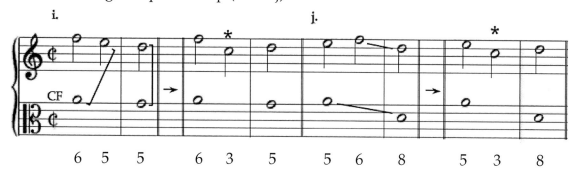

6 5 5   6 3   5   5 6 8   5 3 8

Restrictions on Perfect Consonances:

1) *Identical perfect intervals (p.5 or p.8)* on successive strong beats ("accented-"5ths or 8ves) are forbidden.

   Since the second half note is essentially an embellishing tone, the basic contrapuntal framework is formed by the tones that occur on the strong beats. If the removal of the second half note would result in a first-species example of parallel perfect intervals, this would still be apparent in second species. The occurrence of two identical perfect intervals on successive strong beats should therefore be avoided (see ex. k).

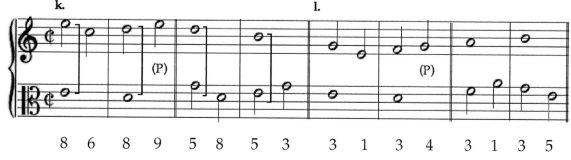

8 6 8 9   5 8 5 3   3 1 3 4   3 1 3 5

2) *Mid-phrase unisons on the first half note of a measure* would produce the same result in second as in first species and *are excluded. Unisons on the second half note of a measure,* however, are sufficiently unaccented and *are acceptable if they are left by step-*

wise motion in the opposite direction from which they are approached (ex. l). Use them sparingly.

Beginning and Ending the Exercise:

Beginning Exercises: The counterpoint may begin with a measure containing two half notes (ex. m) or with a half rest followed by a half note (ex. n). In either case, the first harmonic interval must be a p.1, p.5 or p.8 if the counterpoint is above or a p.1 or p.8 if the counterpoint is below, as it would be in first species..

Ending Exercises: The final tonic will sound inconclusive if it falls on a weak beat. The last measure, therefore, must contain a whole note in both CF and counterpoint. The measure before last will usually contain two half notes in the counterpoint just like any other measure (ex. o). Occasionally, however, the construction of a particular CF or the nature of the counterpoint up to that point will make it necessary to employ a whole note in the next-to-last measure of the counterpoint (see ex. p).

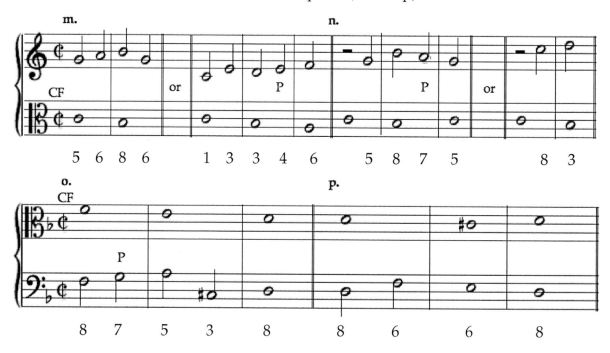

As in first species, the final tonic should be approached by step and in contrary motion with scale-degree 2 in one part and the leading tone in the other.

If scale-degree 2 is in the CF, the note preceding the last note of the counterpoint should be the leading tone. If the CF contains the leading tone the note preceding the last in the counterpoint should be scale-degree 2. If the leading tone is in the CF it should not be duplicated in the counterpoint within that measure. In minor, it will be necessary to alter the seventh note of the natural minor scale to provide the leading tone. It may also be necessary to raise scale-degree 6 to avoid a melodic augmented second.

– Unit Four –

Two-Part Counterpoint: Third Species

All general principles of melodic and contrapuntal writing discussed to this point still apply. This species differs from first and second species only in these particulars:

Rhythmic Organization:

Four-Notes-Against-One (4:1) Four notes in the counterpoint to one note in the CF (Three-Notes-Against-One is also possible, but will not be employed here).

Meter: $\frac{2}{2}$ (₵)

Durational Values (general character): each tone of *cantus firmus* (CF) equals a whole note, each tone of counterpoint equals a quarter note.

Metric organization: simple duple meter, resulting two levels of accented and unaccented tones in counterpoint: the first quarter is strong, the third quarter is accented (but less than the first), and the second and fourth quarters are weak.

Accent:	Strongest	Weak	Strong	Weakest
Quarter:	1	2	3	4

Harmonic Materials Available in this Species:

Consonant Intervals: p.1, p.5 (12), p.8, M.3 (10), m.3 (10), M.6, and m.6.
Dissonant Intervals: M.2 (9), m.2 (9), p.4 (11), a.4 (11), d.5 (12), M.7, m.7
                    available only as passing tones, dissonant neighbor tones, and
                    within *cambiata* and double neighbor figures (see below).

New Harmonic/Melodic Possibilities:

As in second species, the first tone of each measure must be consonant with the CF. Any of the other three quarter notes, however, may be dissonant. The dissonant passing tone is retained much as it was in second species, but new types of dissonance are added as well, including the dissonant neighbor tone and several other compound figures that combine more than one neighbor or neighbor and passing tones together into an ornamental unit.

Basic Definitions:

Passing Tones in Third Species: The first quarter note of each measure must be consonant with the CF. A passing tone may appear, however, on any one of the other quarters (exx. a-c). In each case, the passing tone functions much as it does in second species with the tones on either side of it being consonant with the CF.

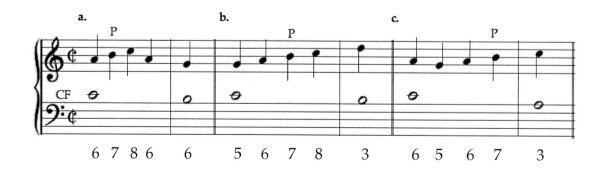

While a dissonant passing tone will occur between two consonant tones in almost every case, certain melodic patterns will occasionally result in two successive dissonant passing tones. This usually occurs when scale degrees 7 and 4 of a major key or 2 and 6 of a minor key appear together, one in the counterpoint and the other in the CF (exx. d and e). In each of these examples, the tone on the second and third quarters both represent dissonances. Their role as step-wise connections between the first and fourth quarters is quite evident, however, allowing us to perceive the passing function of these dissonances quite clearly. These melodic patterns may be employed like any other passing motion.

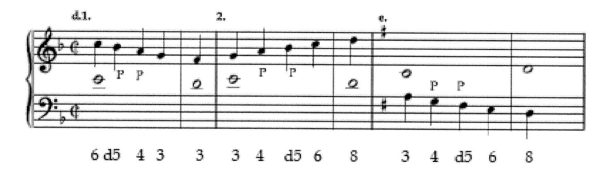

Dissonant Neighbor Tone (N): A neighbor tone is a melodic embellishment in which a relatively unstable tone decorates two occurrences of the same relatively more stable tone by moving away from it by step and then returning to it. A neighbor tone may occur either above or below the primary tone. In third species, both consonant and dissonant neighbor tones may be used. Dissonant neighbors may occur in the counterpoint on any of the last three quarters of a measure. A dissonant neighbor may not occur on the first quarter of a measure (see ex. f).

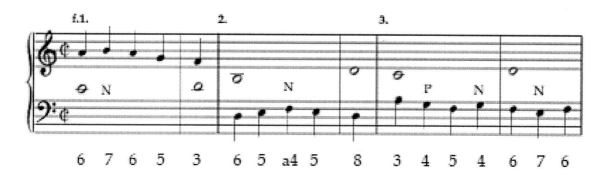

Incomplete Neighbor Tone (**IN**): An incomplete neighbor tone is a neighbor tone that is connected to only one statement of the more stable tone upon which it is dependent. It moves either to that tone or away from it (but not both). It may be approached or left by skip, and is available in species counterpoint only as part of larger melodic figures (see exx. g-j)

Double-Neighbor Pattern (**DN**): A melodic pattern in which two neighbor tones, one above the primary tone and one below (both incomplete) occur in succession as a decoration of that primary tone. They appear together between two statements of the same primary tone, which occur on the first and fourth quarter of the same measure. Either the upper neighbor or the lower neighbor may occur first, but the pattern should be followed by step-wise motion that continues in the direction of the resolution of the second neighbor (see exx g and h)..

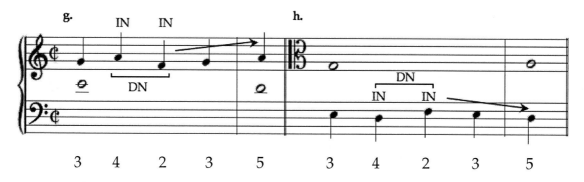

Nota Cambiata **Figures** (**Camb**): This figure combines a passing motion with an incomplete neighbor tone. It is usually considered to contain five notes and embellishes a step-wise motion between the first notes of two successive measures. In this figure, the step-wise resolution of a passing tone (which is almost always dissonant) is interrupted by the insertion of an incomplete neighbor tone (which must be consonant) between the passing tone and its resolution. This incomplete neighbor approaches the tone of resolution from the opposite direction, resulting in a skip of a third between the passing tone and the incomplete neighbor (ex. i). The figure is then completed with a step-wise continuation of the motion in the same direction as that leading from the incomplete neighbor to the tone of resolution (ex. j).

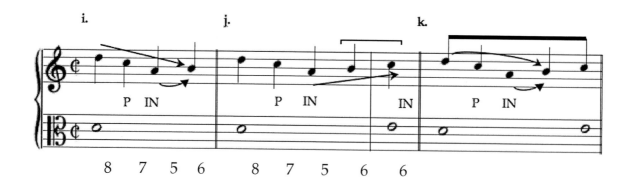

To function correctly, the figure must begin on the first quarter of one measure and end on the first quarter of the next with all the tones of the figure being consonant except for the passing (second) quarter note. Example k illustrates a view of the source of this melodic pattern as an embellishment of a passing motion. This figure may occur in either a descending or an ascending direction, though descending is considerably more common.

Because both the incomplete neighbor and its resolution must be consonant, they must form a 5-6 or 6-5 intervallic pattern with the *cantus firmus*. Similar melodic pattern may appear at times forming different intervallic patterns with the *cantus firmus* (such as 5-6-8-7, where the 7th is formed by a passing or neighbor tone) but these are not considered *nota cambiata* figures.

Restrictions on Perfect Consonances:

As in all previous species, successive perfect consonances of the same type are prohibited. Care must also be taken to avoid too much emphasis on perfect intervals, particularly those that occur on the first quarter of a measure. Fifths, octaves, and unisons in which one occurs on the first quarter of a measure and only one quarter note intervenes (on the third and first or first and third quarters) are prohibited; they are like the accented fifths and octaves of second species and do not sufficiently eliminate the impression of parallels (ex. l). Fifths or octaves with two intervening quarters (from first to fourth or second to first) are permissible, however, if the perfect interval is not too strongly emphasized (ex. m).

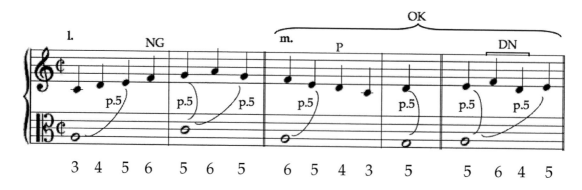

Perfect octaves or fifths with three intervening tones (on the first quarter of successive measures) are permissible. But no more than two successive downbeats should contain the same perfect interval (ex. n). Fifths or octaves that occur on weak quarter notes (second or fourth) may occur with only one intervening quarter note (e.g., on the fourth and second quarters of two successive measures: ex. o).

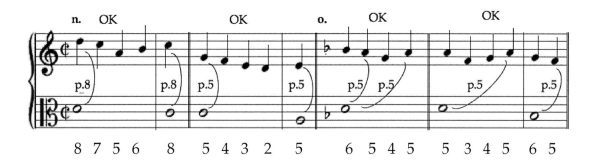

Beginning and ending the exercise:

Beginning Exercises: The counterpoint may begin with a measure containing four quarter notes (ex. p) or with a quarter rest followed by three quarter notes (ex. q). In either case, the first harmonic interval must be a p.1, p.5 or p.8 if the counterpoint is above or a p.1 or p.8 if the counterpoint is below, as it would be in previous species.

Ending Exercises: The final tonic will sound inconclusive if it falls on a weak beat. The last measure, therefore, must contain a whole note in both CF and counterpoint. The measure before last will usually contain four quarter notes in the counterpoint just like any other measure (ex. r). Frequently, these four quarter notes will form a double-neighbor pattern that decorates the leading tone. If such a pattern occurs in minor, it will be necessary to chromatically raise the sixth note of the scale (the lower of the two neighbor notes) to avoid a melodic augmented second in the counterpoint (ex. s).

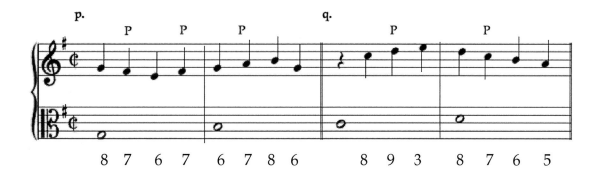

As in first and second species, the final tonic should be approached by step and in contrary motion with scale-degree 2 in one part and the leading tone in the other.

If scale-degree 2 is in the CF, the note preceding the last note of the counterpoint should be the leading tone. If the CF contains the leading tone the note preceding the last in the counterpoint should be scale-degree 2. If the leading tone is in the CF it should not be duplicated in the counterpoint within that measure.

As in earlier species, it will be necessary to alter the seventh note of the natural minor scale to provide the leading tone, and it may be necessary to raise scale-degree 6 as well to avoid a melodic augmented second between it and the leading tone.

In leading to a cadence in a minor key, if the counterpoint contains a double-neighbor pattern that includes a chromatically altered leading tone, the leading tone must appear both as the first and last note of the pattern, that is: on the first and last quarters of the measure (see ex. s). In such an instance, the lower neighbor of the double-neighbor pattern will also have to be raised, providing the raised scale-degree 6, to avoid a melodic augmented second.

– Unit Five –

Two-Part Counterpoint: Fourth Species

All general principles of melodic and contrapuntal writing discussed to this point still apply. This species differs from the preceding ones only in these particulars:

Rhythmic Organization:

Two-Notes-Against-One (2:1), produced as a variant of 1:1 in which the tones of the counterpoint are syncopated against the tones of the CF so that they are attacked on the second, rather than first, beat of each measure.

Meter: $\frac{2}{2}$ (¢)

Durational Values (general character): each tone of cantus firmus (CF) equals a whole note, each tone of counterpoint equals a half note. Most will be tied to another half note (total duration, a whole note).

Harmonic Materials Available in this Species:

Consonant Intervals: p.1, p.5 (12), p.8, M.3 (10), m.3 (10), M.6, and m.6.
Dissonant Intervals: M.2 (9), m.2 (9), p.4 (11), a.4 (11), d.5, M.7, m.7
       available only as suspensions (see below).

New Harmonic/Melodic Possibilities:

In this species, the counterpoint moves in half notes with the half note on the second beat tied to that on the first beat of the following measure. This occurs against a CF that moves in whole notes. In our discussion of second species, we found that the first note of each measure had to be consonant while the second note could be either consonant or a dissonant passing tone. In this species, the reverse is true; *the second half note of each measure must be consonant while the first may be either consonant or dissonant.*

Basic Definitions:

Syncopation: The employment of a rhythmic (dynamic, melodic, or agogic) accent at a metrically weak position in such a way that it contradicts the normal metrical accent. In fourth species this occurs when a note is attacked on a metrically weak beat (the second) and held through a metrically strong beat (the first beat of the following measure). The emphasis on the second beat, produced by an attack on that beat, combined with the de-emphasis of the next first beat, produced by the lack of an attack on it, contradict the normal metrical accent.

The employment of syncopations in fourth species produces a texture that appears to be adapted from first species. Examples a and b show a typical first-species progression and the fourth species progression that results when the counterpoint is shifted through syncopation. While this relationship between first and fourth species is undeniable, every progression in one species can not automatically be converted to a satisfactory progression in the other.

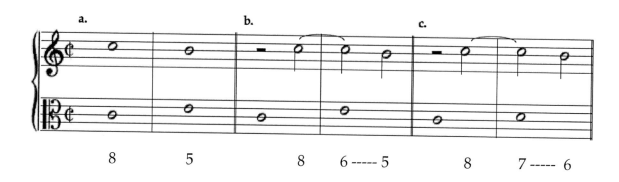

The rhythmic displacement caused by syncopation results in new intervallic relationships between the counterpoint and the CF. In each case, an interval is produced on the first beat of the second measure that would not be present in first species. This interval may be consonant (as in ex. b), or it may be dissonant (as in ex. c). If it is dissonant, it must be handled in a very specific manner or it will not be permitted.

Suspension: A suspension is a *dissonance* produced as the result of a syncopation in which a tone that is consonant against one tone in the CF is carried over against another tone in the CF with which it is dissonant. Unlike passing and neighbor tones, suspensions are inextricably associated with a specific rhythmic footing. Since they are produced by syncopation, they may occur *only in accented metrical positions*.

In all suspensions, the dissonant note in the counterpoint *must resolve downward by step* into a consonant interval against the CF. Properly handled suspension, contain three essential elements: the *preparation*, the *suspension*, and the *resolution*. Example d illustrates these elements.

The *preparation* is the consonant note on the second beat of a measure that is tied over to form the dissonance.

The *suspension* is the dissonance itself.

The *resolution* is the consonant tone to which the suspension moves by descending step-wise motion.

The pattern, *preparation-suspension-resolution* corresponds to an intervallic pattern of *consonance-dissonance-consonance* and a metrical pattern of *weak-strong-weak.*

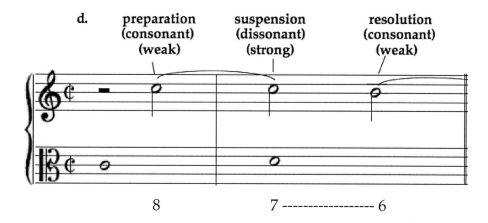

A few words about the necessity of a *downward* resolution are appropriate. To date, no one has yet given an adequate rational explanation for the need to resolve suspensions downward by step. Some have tried to correlate descending motion with relaxation and ascending motion with an increase in tension and explain the need to resolve downward with a need for relaxation after the tension of a suspension. While this seems true enough, it is not sufficient to justify such a severe restriction.

The best explanation can be found in observation. Throughout musical history, composers and listeners have simply found downward resolutions to be more generally satisfying than upward ones (this may be verified by the fact that they occur in overwhelming preponderance throughout the music of the 16th-19th centuries). Since species counterpoint represents an abstraction of the basic principles of counterpoint throughout this period, it seems appropriate to include this matter of consensus as one of its principles.

While upward resolving suspensions do occur, these usually involve leading tones, tones that have strong tendencies to ascend as one of their basic properties. Since these represent the exception rather than the rule, they are not permitted in species counterpoint.

Summary of Contrapuntal Treatment in Fourth Species:

1) The second half note in each measure *must* be consonant with the CF.
2) The first half note of each measure may be either consonant or dissonant. If it is dissonant, it must be tied over from a consonance on the second beat of the preceding measure and must be treated as a proper suspension.

3) The dissonant suspension on the first beat must resolve downward by step into a consonance on the second beat. A consonance on the first beat is free to move either by step or leap in either direction to another consonant tone.

Dissonant Suspensions in Counterpoint Above:

Theoretically, four types of dissonant suspensions are possible with a counterpoint above (exx. e-h): a seventh resolving to a sixth (7-6), a fourth resolving to a third (4-3), a ninth resolving to an octave (9-8), and a second resolving to a unison (2-1, the simple form of the compound 9-8). Not all of these are equally good, however. In general, suspensions that resolve to an imperfect consonance (7-6 and 4-3) are most useful. The perfect intervals that result in the other cases can be disturbing, especially after a dissonance, and can lead to other problems (discussed below). They (especially the 2-1) are best reserved for emergencies or, at least, kept to a minimum.

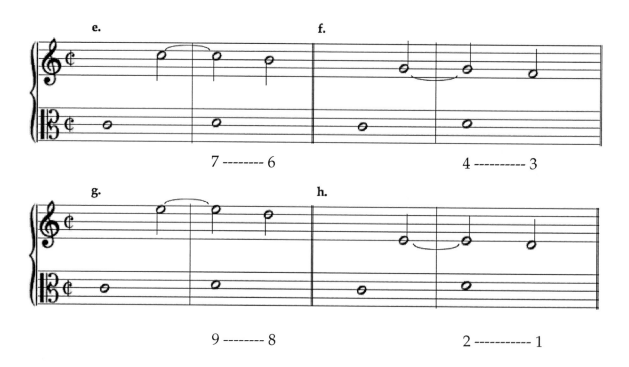

Dissonant Suspensions in Counterpoint Below:

Theoretically, four types of dissonant suspensions are typically possible with a counterpoint below (exx. i-l): a second resolving to a third (2-3), a fourth resolving to a fifth (4-5), a seventh resolving to an octave (7-8) and a ninth resolving to a tenth (9-10, the compound form of 2-3). A fifth form, a diminished fifth resolving to a sixth (d.5-6), is also possible, but less common (ex. m). Here, even more than with the counterpoint above, suspensions that resolve into perfect intervals are weak.

The 4-5 suspension gives rise to the impression of parallel fifths when two occur in succession (more about this below). Even when it occurs alone, the resolution into a perfect consonance is disruptive. It should be used only in an emergency.

The 7-8 suspension is forbidden entirely. This is due to the anticipation of the tone of resolution in the upper voice. While this is also true of the 9-8 and 2-1 suspensions with a counterpoint above (a feature that adds to the weakness of these progressions), it is even more disturbing when the suspension is below and is unacceptable.

All resolutions into imperfect consonances (2-3, 9-10 and d5-6) are permitted freely. Obviously, there are greater restrictions and fewer opportunities for dissonant suspensions to occur with a counterpoint below. Counterpoints below are thus more dependent upon (and will contain a greater number of) consonant syncopations than counterpoints above the CF.

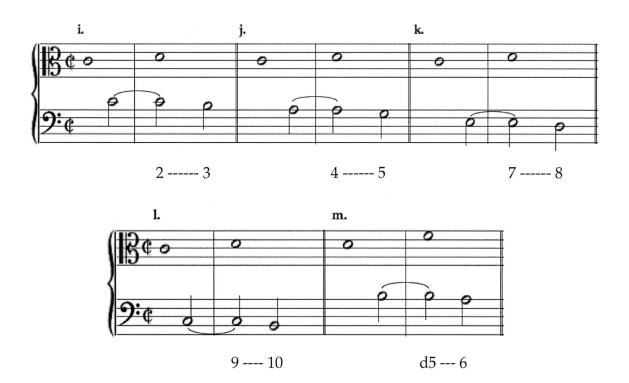

Consonant Syncopations:

Since all dissonant suspensions must resolve downward by step, the only source of ascending step-wise motion or motion by leap is the consonant syncopation. Any consonant interval that occurs on a strong beat may be left by step or by skip in either direction. Among the most significant of these are those that form repeating patterns involving alternations of fifths and sixths. Examples n-q show four patterns created by such alternations. These 5-6 and 6-5 patterns are completely acceptable and may be used as a primary resource for melodic and harmonic variety. Several notes of caution are needed, however.

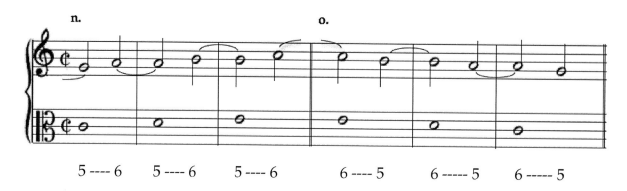

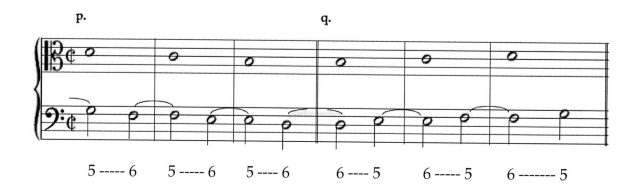

1) Too many repetitions of any pattern are monotonous. Thus, none of these should appear more than three times in a row.

2) *Beware of the diminished fifth.* The diminished fifth is not a consonance yet it may easily sneak into these patterns if one is not careful. Its appearance in a descending 5-6 pattern with the counterpoint below (like ex. p) forms no problem because it would automatically be treated correctly as a suspension. But its occurrence in any of the other patterns would be incorrect, since it would appear in a position reserved for consonances.

3) When reduced to first species, either 6-5 pattern would result in parallel fifths. This makes the fifths in these progressions somewhat more obvious. They should, therefore, be used more sparingly. (Note: this method of avoiding parallel fifths was familiar to composers of many periods. It thus forms the basis of many contrapuntal and harmonic procedures found in common-practice tonal music.)

Syncopations in Series:

The consonant 5-6 and 6-5 progressions are not the only consonant syncopations, nor are they the only syncopations that can appear in series. The remaining consonant syncopations all produce leaps (since no other consonances have tones a step away that are also consonant against the same CF tone). They, therefore, are much less useful in repeating patterns. They are, however, an effective means of changing direction and should be used for that purpose. A series of similar suspensions (e.g., 7-6-7-6, or 9-10-9-10), however, is quite possible and can be very effective. They should not extend beyond three repetitions, though, as this would become too predictable and monotonous. Syncopations in series result in successions of similar voice leading patterns, transposed at successive similar intervals. This kind of procedure is known as a *Sequence*. While similar repetitions of voice-leading patterns are possible in any species, fourth species is the only one in which sequences are permitted.

Melodic Organization:

The nature of fourth species is such that it produces a predominantly descending step-wise motion as a matter of course. One must, therefore, look for opportunities to produce a more interesting melodic line through occasional leaps (possible only through consonant syncopations) and the use of 5-6 and 6-5 ascending patterns.

Restrictions on Perfect Consonances:

Fifths and Octaves:

Because of the nature of fourth species, directly successive equivalent perfect intervals are impossible as long as the pattern of syncopation is maintained. Some intervallic patterns, however, can emphasize recurrences of the same perfect interval in such a way that an impression of successive perfect fifths or octaves is produced. These must be avoided.

In general, consonances that appear between two occurrences of the same perfect interval are more effective in concealing potential parallelisms than are dissonances. Because dissonant suspensions are dependent upon the consonances that surround them for their function, they cannot adequately distract from the occurrence of the same perfect interval in two successive measures. Patterns like 8-9-8, 5-4-5, 1-2-1, 8-7-8 must, therefore, be avoided (exx. r-s)

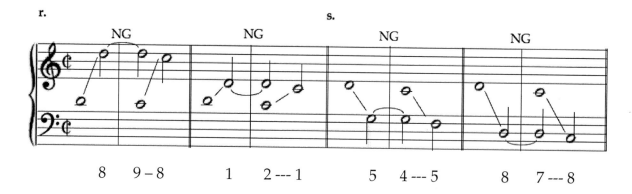

Perfect fifths, octaves, or unisons that are separated by consonant intervals, however, present a different case. In these instances, the consonances between the similar perfect intervals sufficiently distract from them so that they no longer suggest consecutive perfect intervals. Patterns like 8-10-8, 5-6-5, 5-3-5, 1-3-1, etc., are, thus, perfectly acceptable (exx. t-u).

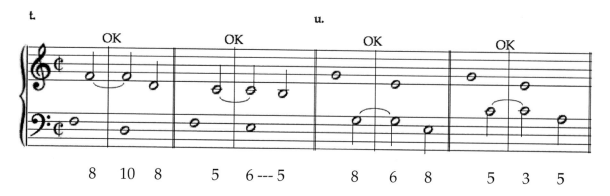

Unisons in Fourth Species:

In fourth species, the rhythmic independence of the voices eliminates any possibility that a unison in the middle of a phrase can be misconstrued as a cadence. Unisons may, therefore, occur freely at any point, even on an accented beat. In general, however, unisons should be avoided as the interval of resolution in a suspension (as in a 2-1 suspension above) because of the anticipation of the tone of resolution (see "Dissonant Suspensions . . .," pp. 22-23). But even these are permissible in an emergency.

Beginning and Ending the Exercise:

Beginning Exercises:

Beginning the exercise offers no problems. All exercises should begin with a half rest followed by a note in the counterpoint that forms a perfect consonance with the CF. The syncopation pattern should then continue unbroken to the cadence. As before, the most useful beginning consonances above are the octave and the fifth; the most useful below are the unison and the octave (exx. v and w).

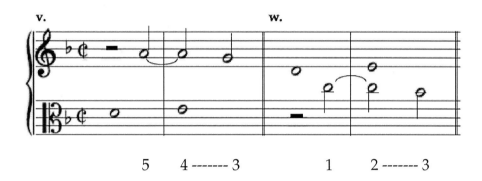

5   4 ------- 3   1   2 ------- 3

Ending Exercises:

As with earlier species, the final measure will contain a whole note in both CF and counterpoint and the measure before last will be typical of the rest of the exercise: that is, it will contain a syncopation (probably a suspension) and its resolution. It will also contain the leading tone in one voice and scale-degree 2 in the other. The second-to-last note will be a half note that is not tied over.

When the leading tone occurs in the counterpoint (the most typical pattern), it will be approached by a 7-6 suspension in a counterpoint above or a 2-3 (9-10) suspension in a counterpoint below (exx. x and y). When the leading tone occurs in the CF, the scale-degree 2 will be approached by a 4-3 suspension in a counterpoint above or by a 5-6 syncopation in a counterpoint below (exx. z and zz).

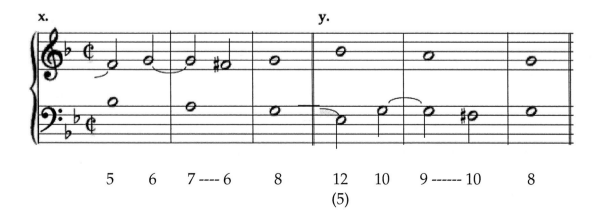

5   6   7 ---- 6   8   12   10   9 ------ 10   8
(5)

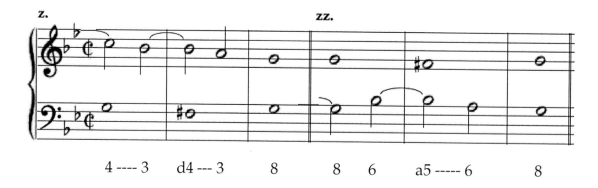

As in the earlier species, the final tonic should be approached by step and in contrary motion with scale-degree 2 in one part and the leading tone in the other. If scale-degree 2 is in the CF, the note preceding the last note of the counterpoint should be the leading tone.

If the CF contains the leading tone the note preceding the last in the counterpoint should be scale-degree 2. If the leading tone is in the CF it should not be duplicated in the counterpoint within that measure.

In minor, it will be necessary to alter the seventh note of the natural minor scale to provide the leading tone, and it may also be necessary to raise scale-degree 6 to avoid a melodic augmented second between it and the leading tone.

Broken Species:

Some theorists allow temporary interruptions of the fourth-species pattern as a way of avoiding extended counterpoint melodies that move entirely in one direction and the problems this may cause. This process can also help avoid a situation in which a suspension would be unable to resolve properly, because it would create a dissonant interval on a weak beat or otherwise unacceptable voice-leading pattern (such as parallel octaves or fifths). Such an interruption occurs when a single measure of second species is introduced within an otherwise fourth species context. This type of event is called "Broken Species."

The measures preceding such an event proceed in normal fourth-species manner with the second note of each measure being consonant as if preparing a syncopation or suspension, but it is not tied over into the next measure, thus "breaking" the species. The note that follows is treated as if it were the first note of a measure in second species: that is, it must be consonant and may be left by either step or skip. The measure proceeds as if it were in second species, except that the second note of that measure must also be consonant (in other words, not a dissonant passing tone) so that it can serve as the preparation of a suspension or syncopation that will be carried over into the next measure, as it would normally be in fourth species. The exercise then proceeds in fourth species as if the "break" had not occurred. Example aa illustrates how such a break might be included in a counterpoint above and example bb illustrates one in a counterpoint below. Instances of broken species are indicated BR in the examples.

aa.

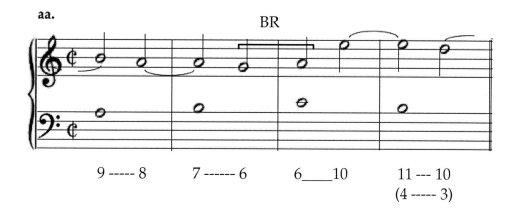

9 ----- 8   7 ------ 6   6___10   11 --- 10
                                          (4 ----- 3)

bb.

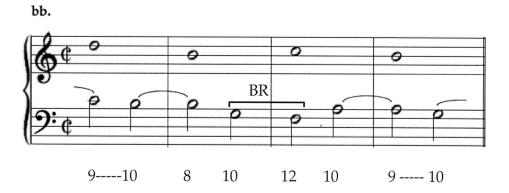

9-----10   8   10   12   10   9 ----- 10

Because too many such interruptions would destroy the basic quality and effect of fourth species, broken species may be included only once in an exercise.

Broken species may be particularly useful as a way to approach a cadence. In such a case, the exercise proceeds as normal in fourth species up the penultimate measure before the cadence. That final measure does not begin with a tied not, but with a "break" in the species followed by two half notes in second species to produce a step-wise approach to the tonic. This occurs most commonly when the counterpoint approaches the cadence from below providing the leading, preceded by the 6th scale degree as counterpoint to scale-degree 2 in the CF. Example cc illustrates how this might occur.

cc.

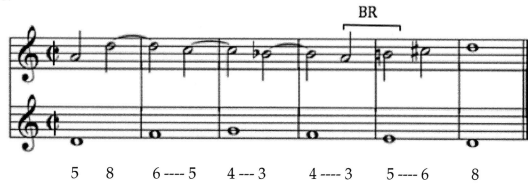

5   8   6 ---- 5   4 --- 3   4 ---- 3   5 ---- 6   8

– Unit Six–

Two-Part Counterpoint: Fifth Species

Fifth species is the culmination in the study of two-part species counterpoint. It blends the most useful and expressive features of each of the four preceding species into a coherent and musically satisfying whole.

All the durational values of the preceding species are represented and are combined in a relatively flexible way (the only exception is the whole note of first species, which is confined to the final measure, the cadence; its appearance elsewhere would disrupt the smooth rhythmic flow and continuity that is the essence of fifth species). Each durational value is governed by the principles of the species in which it previously occurred: half notes, by second (and fourth) species, quarter notes by third species, tied half notes by fourth species, etc. In addition, eighth notes are added as an extension of third species (but tightly restricted).

The use of varied durational values makes it possible to construct melodies of greater complexity and aesthetic quality. It also makes it easier to achieve counterpoint that is merely "correct" (i.e., violates no restrictions in its use of dissonance, voice leading, etc.) in fifth species than in any other species. Consequently, the student should devote a larger portion of his/her efforts to the composition of musically satisfying, not just musically correct, counterpoint.

Rhythmic Organization:

Varied, combining elements of all previous species.

Meter: $\frac{2}{2}$ ($\mathbb{C}$)

Durational Values (general character): Each tone of CF equals a whole note, each tone of counterpoint may equal a half, quarter or eighth note, as allowed under the principles discussed below.

Metric Organization: Simple duple meter, with accent patterns like those of third species combined with weaker, but no less significant agogic accents (accents produced by the relatively longer duration of one tone as compared with those immediately surrounding it).

Harmonic Material Available in this Species:

Consonant Intervals: p.l, p.5 (12), p.8, M.3 (10), m.3 (10), M.6, and m.6.
Dissonant Intervals: p.4 (11), a.4 (11), d.5, M.7, m.7, M.9, m.9. and some others as long as they are properly handled (as passing tones, neighbor tones, suspensions, etc.).

Unmixed Note Values Within Measures:

Theoretically, at least, it is possible to produce a fifth species exercise in which each successive measure (or group of measures) represents counterpoint that follows only one of the earlier species and contains only the durational values that are normally found in each of the applicable species. While it is certainly possible, and sometimes desirable, to continue for an entire measure with a single durational value, the persistent repetition of this practice for any length of time divides the line into segments, with too little contrast within each section and too much contrast between them: in other words, a melody that is musically unsatisfying and does not exhibit a coherent and well balanced rhythmic and melodic flow. Example a presents such a melody; its segmentation and associated poor musical quality are clear.

Such rhythmic segmentations of a melody should be avoided.

Problems like these do not arise when durational values are mixed and combined in varying ways throughout the melody. For this reason, the same durational value should not continue for longer than two measures (usually substantially less).

Mixed Note Values Within the Measure:

In general, *the best effect is obtained when the mixture of durational values results in a proper correlation between two factors: duration and metrical emphasis.* In any situation where long and short notes appear in close proximity, the long notes receive more emphasis because of their greater duration. This kind of accent is called agogic. The occurrence of agogic accents in an unaccented metrical position produces a conflict between the metrical and durational accents that can obscure the clear rhythmic organization of the melody. Agogic accents, therefore, should be carefully handled so that they coincide (or at least do not conflict) with the metrical accents.

In the simple duple meter we are employing, this means that shorter durations should follow, rather than precede longer ones. In example b, the half note and quarter notes fit together quite logically, since the longer half note falls on the metrically accented first beat and the quarter notes fall on the relatively unaccented second beat. In example c, however, the half note falls on the metrically unaccented second quarter, conflicting with the simple duple meter employed in our exercises and implying and underlying pulse of quarter notes (rather than half notes), a quadruple rather than simple duple meter. Syncopations within the measure, therefore, are forbidden.

In example d, the half note on the second beat is preceded by two quarter notes, resulting in an interruption in the smooth rhythmic flow, produced by the sudden halt on the second quarter of the measure. The second half of the measure should lead towards the next downbeat. Coming after the two quarter notes, this half note blocks the flow into the next measure initiated by the quarters that precede it rather than continues it. Once stopped, the motion begins again with a jolt at the next downbeat, further disrupting the even flow of the melody. This rhythmic pattern may not, therefore be employed. If it were altered in a way that corrected the problems, however, it could be used.

Example e shows how this may be accomplished by tying the half note over into the following measure. With this change, the motion no longer begins abruptly in the next measure; in fact, the syncopation actually helps to continue the momentum into the next measure (especially if it is a suspension, which must resolve on its second beat). Two quarters may thus precede a half note, *but only if the half note is tied over into the following measure.*

Example f presents the rhythmic patterns that employ half and quarter notes, which may occur without problem in fifth species.

Additional Rhythmic Possibilities:

Eighth Notes:
In addition to the combination of durational values from earlier species into rhythmic patterns not available in those species, fifth species makes a new durational value available for use as embellishment of underlying simpler rhythmic patterns: the eighth note. Eighth notes and the rhythmic and voice leading patterns they make possible are unique to fifth species. They must be used sparingly and carefully if the line is not to become too active and instrumental in character. Three principles govern the use of eighth notes:

1) They must occur as part of a pair (two eighth notes at a time), with only one pair per measure.
2) They may occur only on weak quarters, second or fourth, within the measure.
3) They must be approached, move, and be left by step as part of a passing or neighboring motion.

The role of eighth notes is purely decorative. *At no time must they participate in or create essential voice leading* (like the final step-wise motion to the tonic at a cadence), Their placement on the second or fourth quarter requires that they be preceded by a quarter note and thus follows the basic principle that longer values must precede shorter ones. In other words, eighth notes relate to quarter notes as quarter notes relate to half notes and must be treated in an analogous fashion. Examples 9 g and h illustrate two of the many possible correct uses for eighth notes in fifth species. Examples i and j illustrate two of the many possible incorrect uses for eighth notes in fifth species.

Continuation After Syncopations:

In pure fourth species, consonant syncopations occur when a half note on the second beat of one measure is tied to another half note on the first beat of the next measure. In that pure species, rhythmic motion resumes with the second beat (second half note) of the next measure, which initiates another syncopation, thus forming a continuous pattern of fourth-species syncopations that span the entire exercise (ex. k).

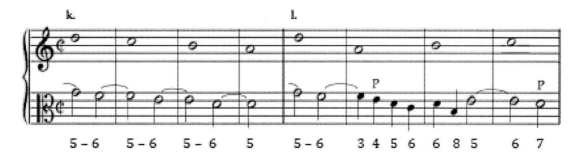

In fifth species, however, a measure containing a fourth-species initiation of a consonant syncopation does not have to be followed by a measure of fourth-species half notes; it could be followed by a measure containing third-species quarter notes. In a case where these quarter notes begin on the first beat of the next measure, the half note of the preceding measure cannot be tied to another half note, but rather must be tied to a quarter note. In fifth species, therefore, consonant syncopations must be initiated by half notes (in accordance with fourth-species principles), but that half note may be tied to a quarter note rather than another half note. Example l illustrates one possible instance of this type of consonant syncopation. Since it is permissible to follow a quarter note at the beginning of a measure with two eighth notes, the resolution of the syncopation in the first measure of example l could have been followed by a quarter and two eighths at the beginning of the next measure, rather than two quarter notes (see example h and example m below).

Some authors extend this principle to allow for the resolution of a suspension (which is, after all, a dissonant syncopation) on the second quarter note as well. While valid in itself, this practice tends to shift the perceived pulse to the level of quarter notes (like the syncopation within the measure of example c). For this reason it is best avoided, and will not be permitted here.

These two additional rhythmic possibilities make additional rhythmic patterns possible within a given measure. Example m. presents the patterns that may be added to those already given in example f. In each case, the first note of the measure may be tied over from a half note in the preceding measure (this is also true of the examples given earlier in example f).

Neither these nor the patterns of example f should be allowed to become motivic. Immediate or persistent repetition of any pattern carries with it the danger of segmentation (like that of example a). While well-spaced repetitions of a recognizable rhythmic pattern may add to the coherence of a melody (and thus would be desirable), too many literal repetitions of a pattern, especially in close proximity to each other, will result in the segmentation of the melody into small melodic cells and will destroy its overall coherence. A careful balance between repetition and contrast is the key, and is one of the hardest musical goals to achieve. Example n presents a melody in which too much literal repetition has destroyed its rhythmic flow and overall unity.

n.

One more point about rhythmic flow needs to be added. In general, smoother continuity results when note values change in the middle of a measure rather than at the beginning. It is easy enough to change from half notes to quarter notes; changing from quarter notes to half notes poses more of a problem (and has already been discussed). Suspensions offer the best means for overcoming this problem. Eighth notes decorate quarter-note motion and need not be counted as a significant change in rhythmic values.

Dissonance Treatment:

The treatment of dissonance in fifth species poses few problems not handled in the course of the earlier species. Each durational value is governed by the principles of the species from which it is derived; half notes must be consonant when on the first beat and may be dissonant on the second beat only if treated as passing tones; quarter notes must be consonant when the first note in a measure, but may form dissonant neighbor tones, passing tones, or other permissible dissonances on the rhythmically appropriate succeeding quarters. Eighth notes pose no problems in dissonance treatment, since they can appear only on weak quarter notes and their requirement of step-wise motion will, itself, insure correct handling of any dissonances that may arise. Either the first or second note of the pair (and occasionally both) may be dissonant, and may appear as either passing or neighbor notes.

The only dissonance that may be slightly modified in its treatment is the suspension. As noted above, the mixture of durational values makes it possible to reduce the normal half-note duration of the second note of a consonant syncopation to a quarter note, so that melodic motion resumes on the second, rather than third quarter of the measure. While the resolution of a suspension cannot be similarly moved to the second quarter of the measure, *it must appear on the third quarter note of the measure*, the duration of dissonant suspension itself may be shortened and a decorating quarter note or pair of eighth notes may be inserted between the suspension (on the first quarter) and its resolution (on the third quarter).

As is standard in fourth species, the suspension procedure spans two measures and incorporates the elements of *preparation, suspension,* and *resolution* in the same way as they appear in fourth species. In fifth species, as in fourth, *the preparation* of a suspension *must be a half note* that takes up the third and fourth quarters of a measure (this is also true of the preparation of a consonant syncopation, as discussed above). This half note is tied over the bar line to become a dissonant suspension, which resolves to a consonance on the third quarter (second half note) of the second measure. In fifth species, unlike fourth however, the suspension itself need not take up the entire first half of the second measure. It may be shortened by the insertion of an embellishment consisting of either a quarter notes or a pair of eighth notes.

Examples o and p present two instances of such a procedure, which is known as a *Decorated Resolution*. In each of these cases, an incomplete neighbor tone is inserted as the second quarter note of the measure, shortening the dissonant suspension, but not displacing the resolution. In example o, an incomplete lower neighbor precedes the resolution, while in example p and incomplete upper neighbor follows the suspension; in both cases, the normal step-wise motion is disturbed by the skip of a third that is produced; in both cases, the underlying half-note pulse and its correlation with the consonant-dissonant-consonant pattern of the suspension remain undisturbed.

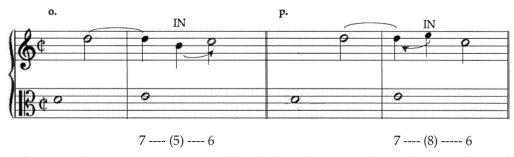

7 ---- (5) ---- 6   7 ---- (8) ----- 6

Examples q and r present two possible elaborations on these decorated resolutions. In each, the skip that was produced by the insertion of the incomplete neighbor is filled in with a passing tone; in example q, the passing tone connects the suspension to the incomplete lower neighbor by step; in example r, the passing tone connects the incomplete upper neighbor to the resolution by step. These types of decoration are even more common than those of examples o and p, because they restore the totally step-wise motion that is typical of the normal treatment of suspensions. Fundamental to the proper understanding of these procedures is a realization and recognition of the relative structural significance and melodic role of each tone.

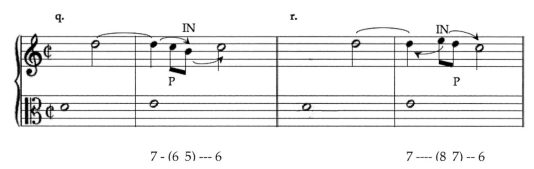

7 - (6 5) --- 6   7 ---- (8 7) -- 6

In q, it might be possible to think of the first eighth note as the resolution of the suspension, followed by a lower neighbor and a repetition of the same tone. In r too, it might be possible to think of the first eighth note as a resolution of the suspension (albeit, an upward one), followed by just another consonant tone. In both cases, however, our expectation of rhythmic continuity resulting from the fundamentally duple metrical division leads us to expect a resolution on the third, not second quarter of the measure; this sense of rhythmic continuity keeps us from hearing these second quarters as resolutions of the suspensions, despite their consonance. The melodic context reinforces this perception. The conjunct passing motions along with their rhythmic placement clearly identify the inserted eighth and quarter notes as embellishments, with the underlying fourth-species half-note motion still remaining part of our conscious perception of the voice leading.

In both examples q and r, the melodic pattern results from the ornamentation, with passing tones, of tones that are themselves ornamentations of the structural tones, the incomplete neighbors. This illustrates in a small way a fundamental truth of musical structure, the existence of structural levels. These tones can best be understood when viewed in relief. If we peel off the most surface layer of structure, the passing tones, we are left with the underlying embellishments, the incomplete neighbors. If we remove the next deepest layer, the incomplete neighbors, we are left with the unadorned suspensions and resolutions, just as they would appear in fourth species.

Our mental ear is aware of the embellishing and more surface role of these decorations even if our conscious ear is not. Because of the transient nature of the decorative tones, our ear hears through the intervening tones and perceives the essential continuity from suspension to resolution. The principle here is the same as that of the *nota cambiata* or double-neighbor notes of third species. On a miniature scale, it represents one of the basic premises of musical structure: that *relationships between non-consecutive tones often take primacy over relationships between immediately consecutive ones.*

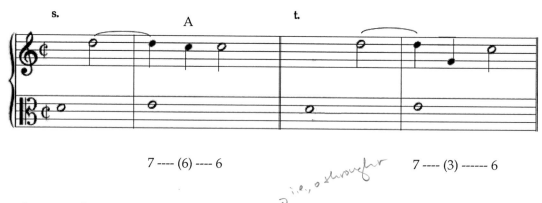

7 ---- (6) ---- 6   7 ---- (3) ------ 6

Examples s and t present two additional types of decorations, both of which are decidedly less common than these first four. In s, the resolution of the suspension is preceded by an anticipation of the tone of resolution. Here in particular, rhythm plays a central role in our perception of the second tone, rather than the first, as the resolution. In t, a tone that is both approached and left by leap is inserted. It is not an incomplete neighbor, a passing tone, nor any other standard type of melodic embellishment. Its acceptability derives from the fact that, like the other quarter-note insertions, it is consonant. This lets the ear perceive it as if it were from a different voice, a third voice that until now had been silent. While obviously no third voice exists, the effect is similar to what we would hear if there were one and is sufficient to allow this as an embellishment.

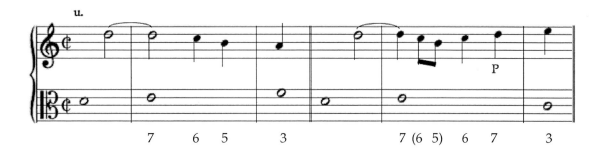

One other point about the resolution needs to be made. While the resolution must occur on the third quarter note (second half note) of the measure, it need not be a half note long. Once it occurs on the third quarter, the resolution can have only a quarter note's duration and be followed by another quarter or two eighths. This is possible because of the unaccented and essentially connective role of the fourth quarter note, which allows us still to correlate this rhythm with the "suspension-on-first-half, resolution-on-second-half" model from fourth species. This is true even in the case of a decorated resolution. Example u presents two of many possibilities.

Restrictions on Perfect Consonances:

As in all earlier species, immediately successive perfect fifths, octaves, and unisons are forbidden. Other considerations of voice leading, like those affecting dissonance treatment, depend upon the particular mixture of durational values employed at any given moment. Octaves and fifths on successive first beats (accented octaves and fifths) are acceptable if they are separated by three quarter notes (as in third species). If only a half note separates them, they are not acceptable (as in second species), because they are not adequately concealed. A mixed rhythm of a half followed by two quarters (ex. v) represents a borderline case. In most instances, it would be acceptable as long as the fifths or octaves are not otherwise emphasized).

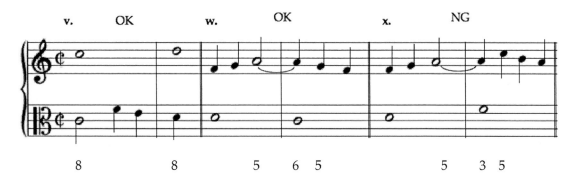

A consonant syncopation lasting only a quarter note can present the possibility of after beat fifths or octaves separated only by one quarter note. When the second interval is approached by step-wise motion (ex. w), the effect is not only acceptable, but can be quite desirable. When the second interval is approached by skip, however, it receives too much emphasis; these progressions should be avoided (ex. X).

Correlation Between Melodic and Rhythmic Motion:

Fifth species, unlike any other, offers us the opportunity to control the rate of melodic motion through variations in rhythm. Example y shows several ways in which a melodic progression might span a sixth between e and c in two measures. The first two examples use pure second and third species, respectively, while the others show ways in which fifth species can be employed. Through rhythmic accents (both metrical and agogic), different tones in each progression are emphasized, and, while the overall shape of the phrase is the same, the details of melodic direction and shape differ significantly.

No one of these other possibilities is inherently better than the others. The choice, as to which to use in a given melody will be determined on the basis of context: which will best complement and continue the overall melodic and rhythmic shape of the melody; which is the most consistent, logical outgrowth of the balance of the melody.

The following guidelines should help you use rhythmic means to best effect in shaping the melodic contour:

1) Extended step-wise motion usually functions as a means of connecting two tones that are of relatively more structural significance within the melody. Longer durational values move these two tones further apart and make it more difficult for the listener to perceive their relationship; they can also slow down the melodic progression to the point that it becomes sluggish. For these reasons, extended step-wise motion should usually be assigned to smaller durational values (quarter and/or eighth notes).
2) For much the same reason, motion that decorates a stationary tone should employ quarter and/or eighth notes. Even if half-note motion would yield proper dissonance treatment, it would produce a relatively static rhythmic effect.

3) In a series of dissonant suspensions, the total distance traversed can be rather small and the rhythmic flow can become static and predictable. For these reasons, a succession of suspensions is usually best handled by embellishing each with some sort of decorated resolution. The decorations should be varied so as not to generate a sequence.

4) It is best to allow melodic and rhythmic momentum to develop gradually as the melody progresses. For this reason, the most active rhythmic features should occur in the central portion, most often at and around the melodic climax. The beginning of the exercise is usually best achieved with larger durational values and conjunct motion. In approaching the melodic climax, rhythm should be accelerated and mare disjunct motion can be effective. Cadences can seem sudden if approached with too much rhythmic activity, so it is best to broaden out the rhythm once again toward the cadence.

5) Because of the vocal nature of species counterpoint, several observations regarding the nature of vocal performance are relevant. Melodic lines that combine high rates of rhythmic activity with predominately disjunct motion are decidedly instrumental in character and should be avoided. In general, leaps present more problems for singers than conjunct motion and often require some time for preparation. Skips are, thus, usually best preceded by longer durational values (half notes): the larger the skip, the more necessary the preparation. Skips, however, often generate an increased sense of momentum and are, therefore, easily followed by increased rates of rhythmic activity.

Beginning and Ending the Exercises:

Beginning Exercises:

As noted above, longer durational are best used at the beginning of an exercise, so openings like those of second or fourth are most effective. Beginning with quarter notes is also possible, but should lead almost immediately to motion in half or you will be left with nothing for the climax. As a rule, openings that include a rest will help to emphasize the independence of the voices. Example z presents three typical and effective openings.

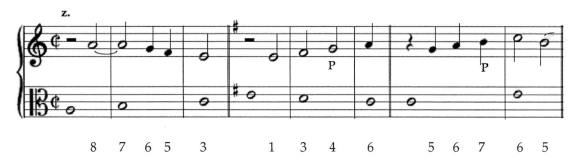

```
    8   7  6  5     3       1   3   4    6       5   6   7    6  5
```

Ending Exercises:

By far the most effective cadences result from a dissonant suspension into the leading tone, as in fourth species. This is typically enhanced through the addition of a decorated resolution. The progression of example zz is typical and represents an exception to the general principle that shorter durations at the beginning of a measure can only be followed by a half note if it is tied over into the next measure.

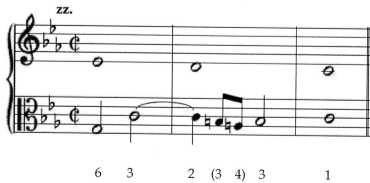

The occurrence of the leading tone, with its inherent melodic tension prevents any sense of arrested melodic motion. This combined with the fact that a tie across the bar line would not allow a cadence, makes this exception quite reasonable. Other cadence patterns are possible, especially if the leading tone is in the CF, but this is by far the most common.

* * * * * * * * * * * * *

This concludes our study of Two-Part Species Counterpoint. Beyond this lies the study of Species Counterpoint in three parts, counterpoint in "Free Species" (Fifth Species in all voices), and counterpoint in various styles, like 16th Century, 18th Century, etc. Alas, all these lie beyond the scope of this text or the course for which it was designed. Students are urged to continue the study of counterpoint throughout their training and careers as a musician, as it is the ultimate source of tonal coherence in every style and genre.

– Exercises –

First Species:

Counterpoint Assignment, no. 1

Name _____

Examine the following excerpt. Locate at least 6 errors in voice leading, melodic writing or harmonic structure. Indicate each by type and measure number in the spaces provided below. Then compose an alternative First Species counterpoints to the *cantus firmus*, on the staff below. Analyze the counterpoint between your new melody and the *cantus firmus*, showing all the harmonic intervals between the two lowest staves.

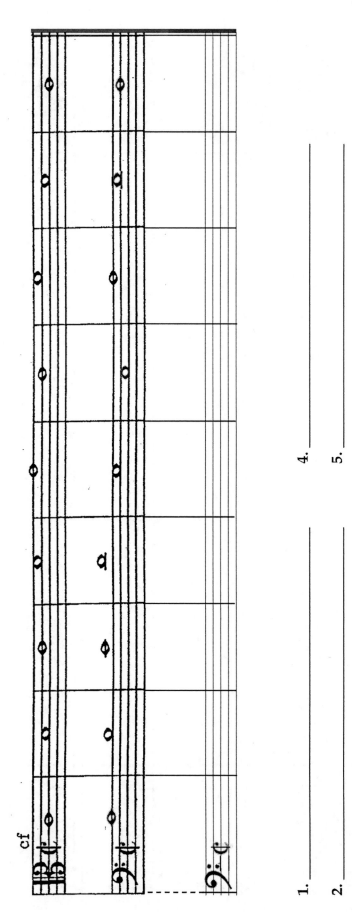

1. _____
2. _____
3. _____

4. _____
5. _____
6. _____

First Species:

Counterpoint Assignment, no. 2

Name _____

Examine the following excerpt. Locate at least 6 errors in voice leading, melodic writing or harmonic structure. Indicate each by type and measure number in the spaces provided below. Then compose an alternative First Species counterpoints to the *cantus firmus*, on the staff below. Analyze the counterpoint between your new melody and the *cantus firmus*, showing all the harmonic intervals between the two lowest staves.

1. _____

2. _____

3. _____

4. _____

5. _____

6. _____

First Species:

Counterpoint Assignment, no. 3

Name _____

Examine the following excerpt. Locate at least 6 errors in voice leading, melodic writing or harmonic structure. Indicate each by type and measure number in the spaces provided below. Then compose an alternative First Species counterpoints to the *cantus firmus*, on the staff above. Analyze the counterpoint between your new melody and the *cantus firmus*, showing all the harmonic intervals between the two highest staves.

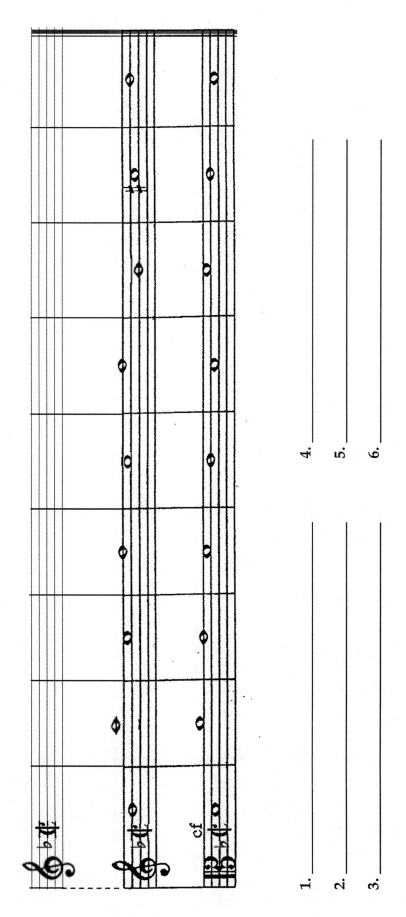

1. _____

2. _____

3. _____

4. _____

5. _____

6. _____

First Species:

Counterpoint Assignment, no. 4

Name _____

Analyze the following excerpt, indicating each harmonic interval between the staves. Then compose two alternative First Species counterpoints to the *cantus firmus*, one above and one below. Analyze the counterpoint with each in the same way.

Counterpoint Assignment, no. 5

Name _____

First Species:

Analyze the following excerpt, indicating each harmonic interval between the staves. Then compose two alternative First Species counterpoints to the *cantus firmus*, one above and one below. Analyze the counterpoint with each in the same way.

First Species: Counterpoint Assignment, no. 6

Name _____

Compose two First-Species counterpoints to the given *cantus firmus*, one above and one below. Refer to Units 1 and 2 of the *Introduction to Two-Part Species Counterpoint* (pp. 1-6) as the examples discussed in class as models. Analyze the passages, showing all harmonic intervals as we did in class.

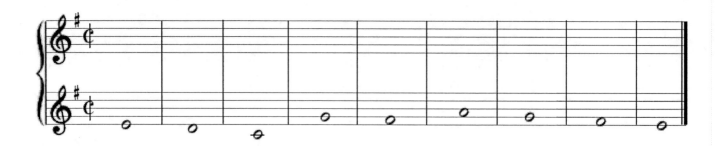

First Species: **Counterpoint Assignment, no. 7**

Name _____

Compose two First-Species counterpoints to the given *cantus firmus*, one above and one below. Refer to Units 1 and 2 of the *Introduction to Two-Part Species Counterpoint* (pp. 1-6) as the examples discussed in class as models. Analyze the passages, showing all harmonic intervals as we did in class.

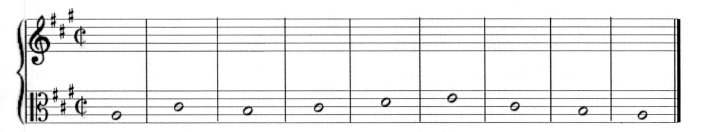

First Species: Counterpoint Assignment, no. 8

Name _____

Compose two First-Species counterpoints to the given *cantus firmus,* one above and one below. Refer to Units 1 and 2 of the *Introduction to Two-Part Species Counterpoint* (pp. 1-6) as the examples discussed in class as models. Analyze the passages, showing all harmonic intervals as we did in class.

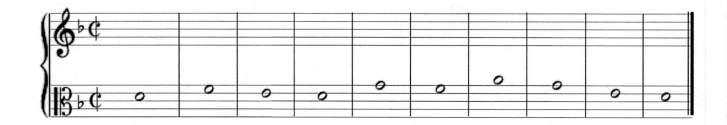

First Species: Counterpoint Assignment, no. 9

Name _____

Compose two First-Species counterpoints to the given *cantus firmus*, one above and one below. Refer to Units 1 and 2 from the *Introduction to Two-Part Species Counterpoint* (pp. 1-6) as the examples discussed in class as models. Analyze the passages, showing all harmonic intervals as we did in class.

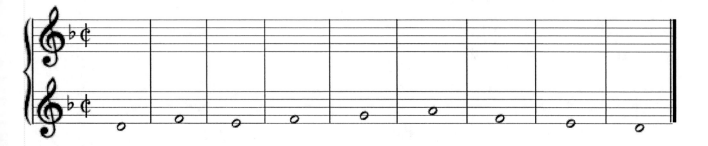

Second Species:

Counterpoint Assignment, no. 1

Name _____

Examine the following excerpt. Locate at least 10 errors in voice leading, melodic writing or harmonic structure. Circle each and indicate each by type and measure number in the spaces provided below. Then compose an alternative Second Species counterpoints to the *cantus firmus*, on the staff above. Analyze the counterpoint between your new melody and the *cantus firmus*, showing all the harmonic intervals between the two highest staves. Identify embellishing tones, like Consonant Passing tones (CP), Dissonant Passing tones (DP), Consonant Neighbor tones (CN), etc. by labeling each according above the note.

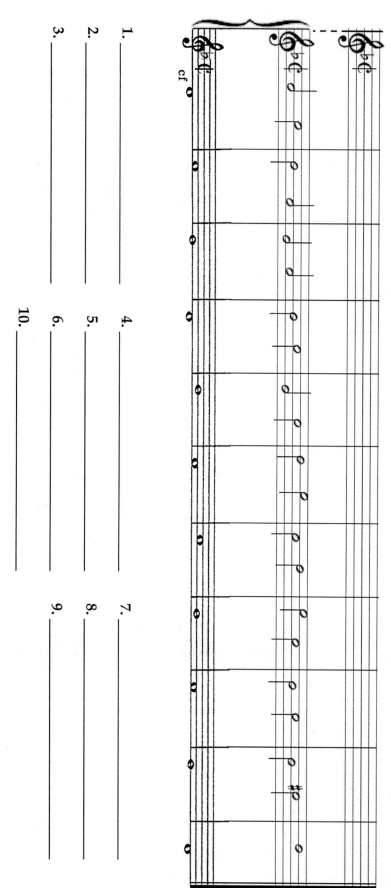

1. _____   7. _____

2. _____   8. _____

3. _____   9. _____

4. _____   10. _____

5. _____

6. _____

Second Species:

Counterpoint Assignment, no. 2

Name _____

Examine the following excerpt. Locate at least 10 errors in voice leading, melodic writing or harmonic structure. Circle each and indicate each by type and measure number in the spaces provided below. Then compose an alternative Second Species counterpoints to the *cantus firmus*, on the staff above. Analyze the counterpoint between your new melody and the *cantus firmus*, showing all the harmonic intervals between the two highest staves. Identify embellishing tones, like Consonant Passing tones (CP), Dissonant Passing tones (DP), Consonant Neighbor tones (CN), etc. by labeling each accordingly above the note.

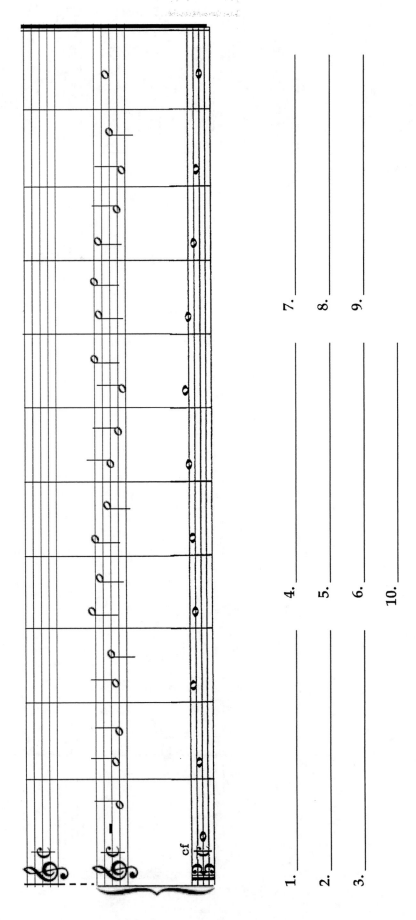

1. _____

2. _____

3. _____

4. _____

5. _____

6. _____

7. _____

8. _____

9. _____

10. _____

Second Species:

Counterpoint Assignment, no. 3

Name _____

Examine the following excerpt. Locate at least 10 errors in voice leading, melodic writing or harmonic structure. Circle each and indicate each by type and measure number in the spaces provided below. Then compose an alternative Second Species counterpoints to the *cantus firmus*, on the staff below. Analyze the counterpoint between your new melody and the *cantus firmus*, showing all the harmonic intervals between the two lowest staves. Identify embellishing tones, like Consonant Passing tones (CP), Dissonant Passing tones (DP), Consonant Neighbor tones (CN), etc. by labeling each according above the note.

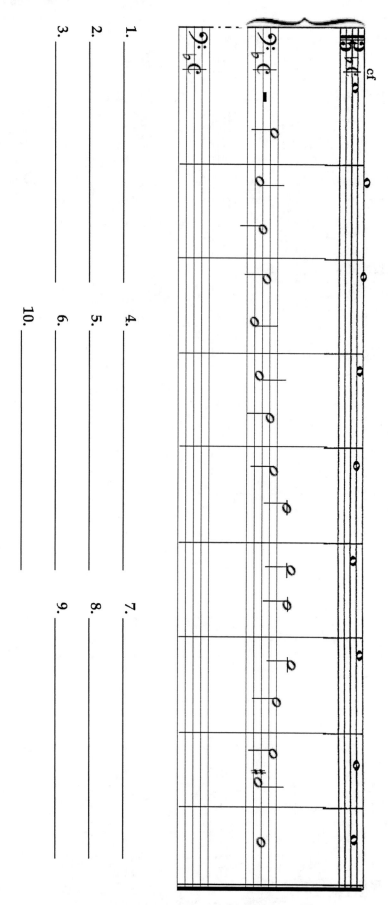

1. _____   4. _____   7. _____

2. _____   5. _____   8. _____

3. _____   6. _____   9. _____

                        10. _____

Second Species:

Counterpoint Assignment, no. 4

Name _____

Analyze the following excerpt, indicating each harmonic interval between the staves and identifying embellishing tones like Dissonant Passing tones (DP), Consonant Passing tones (CP) and Consonant Neighbor tones (CN) in the appropriate manner. Then compose two alternative Second Species counterpoints to the *cantus firmus*, one above and one below. Analyze the counterpoint with each in the same way.

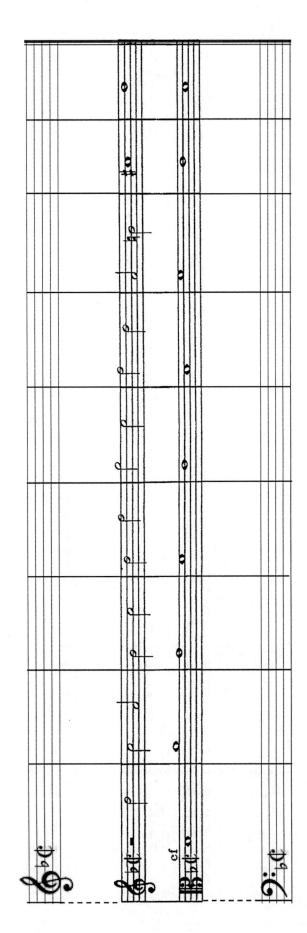

Second Species:

Counterpoint Assignment, no. 5

Name _____

Analyze the following excerpt, indicating each harmonic interval between the staves and identifying embellishing tones like Dissonant Passing tones (DP), Consonant Passing tones (CP) and Consonant Neighbor tones (CN) in the appropriate manner. Then compose two alternative Second Species counterpoints to the *cantus firmus*, one above and one below. Analyze the counterpoint with each in the same way.

Second Species:

Counterpoint Assignment, no. 6

Name _____

Analyze the following excerpt, indicating each harmonic interval between the staves and identifying embellishing tones like Dissonant Passing tones (DP), Consonant Passing tones (CP) and Consonant Neighbor tones (CN) in the appropriate manner. Then compose two alternative Second Species counterpoints to the *cantus firmus*, one above and one below. Analyze the counterpoint with each in the same way.

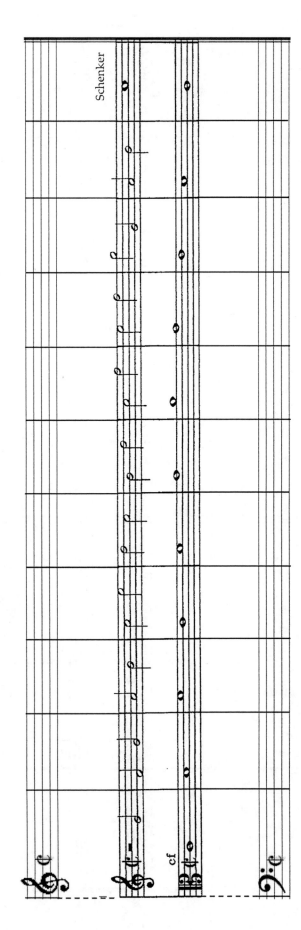

Second Species:

Counterpoint Assignment, no. 7

Name _____

Analyze the following excerpt, indicating each harmonic interval between the staves and identifying embellishing tones like Dissonant Passing tones (DP), Consonant Passing tones (CP) and Consonant Neighbor tones (CN) in the appropriate manner. Then compose two alternative Second Species counterpoints to the *cantus firmus*, one above and one below. Analyze the counterpoint with each in the same way.

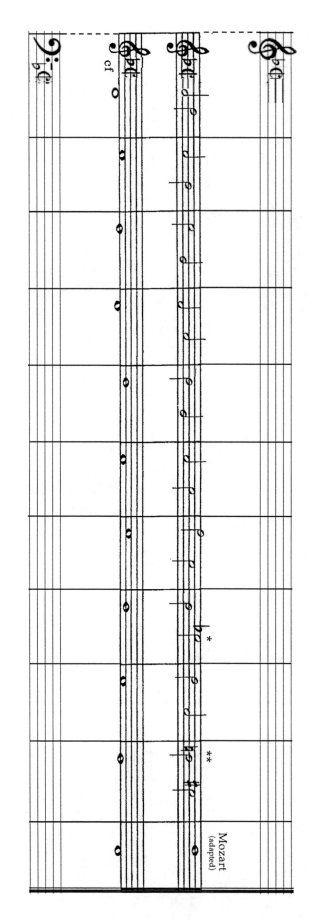

* Why is it E♭ here, even though it is not in the key? What melodic error is it intended to avoid? _____

** Why is this B♮ rather than B♭? What melodic and harmonic errors is it intended to avoid? _____ ,

and _____ .

Second Species:

Counterpoint Assignment, no. 8

Name _____

Compose two Second-Species counterpoints to the given *cantus firmus*, one above and one below. Refer to Units 1, 2, and 3 of the *Introduction to Two-Part Species Counterpoint* (pp. 1-11) and the examples discussed in class as models. Analyze the passages, showing all harmonic intervals as we did in class. Identify all Consonant Passing tones (CP), Dissonant Passing tones (DP) Consonant Neighbor tones (CN) etc., with appropriate abbreviations.

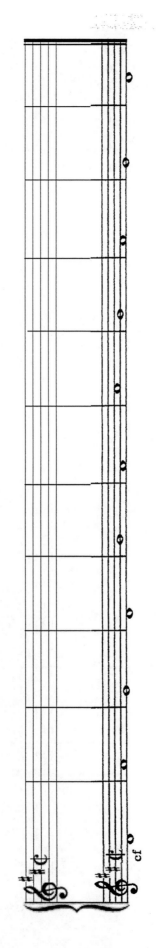

Second Species:

Counterpoint Assignment, no. 9

Name _____

Compose two Second-Species counterpoints to the given *cantus firmus*, one above and one below. Refer to Units 1, 2, and 3 of the *Introduction to Two-Part Species Counterpoint* (pp. 1-11) and the examples discussed in class as models. Analyze the passages, showing all harmonic intervals as we did in class. Identify all Consonant Passing tones (CP), Dissonant Passing tones (DP), Consonant Neighbor tones (CN), etc., with appropriate abbreviations.

cf

cf

Counterpoint Assignment, no. 10

Name _____

Second Species:

Compose two Second-Species counterpoints to the given *cantus firmus*, one above and one below. Refer to Units 1, 2 and 3 of the *Introduction to Two-Part Species Counterpoint* (pp. 1-11) and the examples discussed in class as models. Analyze the passages, showing all harmonic intervals as we did in class. Identify all Consonant Passing tones (CP), Dissonant Passing tones (DP), Consonant Neighbor tones (CN), etc., with appropriate abbreviations.

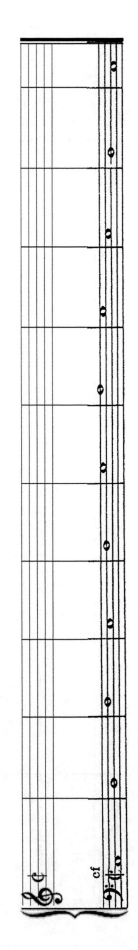

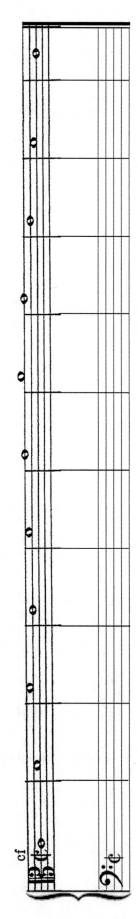

Second Species:

Counterpoint Assignment, no. 11

Name _____

Compose two Second-Species counterpoints to the given *cantus firmus*, one above and one below. Refer to Units 1, 2 and 3 of the *Introduction to Two-Part Species Counterpoint* (pp. 1-11) and the examples discussed in class as models. Analyze the passages, showing all harmonic intervals as we did in class. Identify all Consonant Passing tones (CP), Dissonant Passing tones (DP), Consonant Neighbor tones (CN), etc., with appropriate abbreviations.

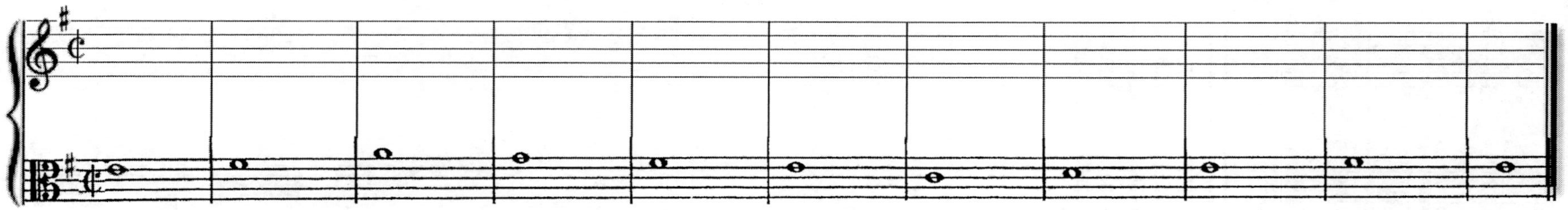

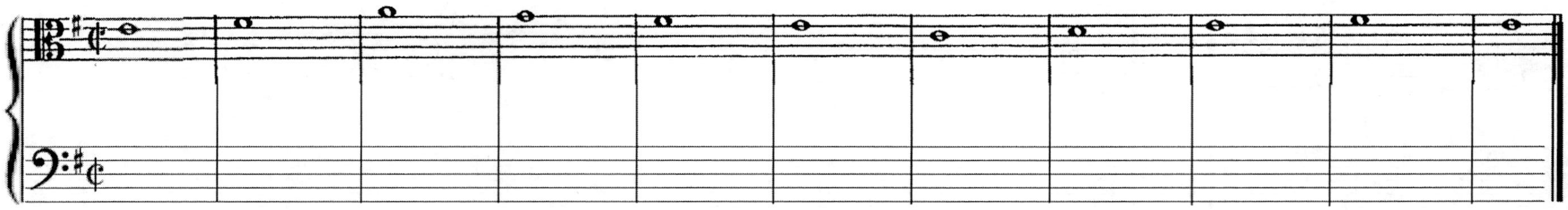

Third Species:

Counterpoint Assignment, no. 1

Name _____

Examine the following excerpt. Locate at least 12 errors in voice leading, melodic writing or harmonic structure. Circle each and indicate each by type and measure number in the spaces provided below. Then compose an alternative Third Species counterpoints to the *cantus firmus*, on the staff above. Analyze the counterpoint between your new melody and the *cantus firmus*, showing all the harmonic intervals between the two highest staves. Identify embellishing tones, like Consonant Passing tones (CP), Dissonant Passing tones (DP), Consonant Neighbor tones (CN), etc. by labeling each accordingly above the note.

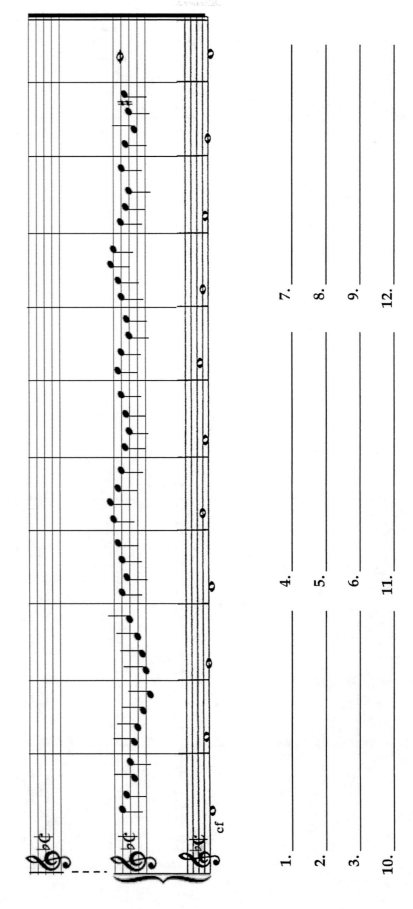

1. _____
2. _____
3. _____
10. _____

4. _____
5. _____
6. _____
11. _____

7. _____
8. _____
9. _____
12. _____

Third Species:

Counterpoint Assignment, no. 2

Name _____

Examine the following excerpt. Locate at least 12 errors in voice leading, melodic writing or harmonic structure. Circle each and indicate each by type and measure number in the spaces provided below. Then compose an alternative Third Species counterpoints to the *cantus firmus*, on the staff above. Analyze the counterpoint between your new melody and the *cantus firmus*, showing all the harmonic intervals between the two highest staves. Identify embellishing tones, like Consonant Passing tones (CP), Dissonant Passing tones (DP), Consonant Neighbor tones (CN), etc. by labeling each accordingly above the note.

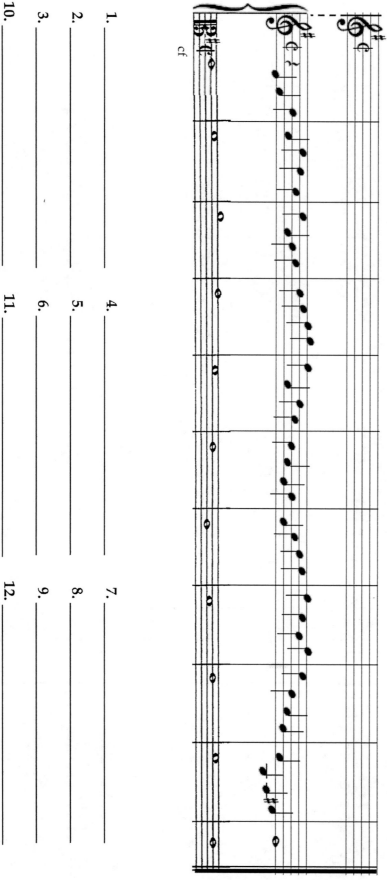

1. _____   4. _____   7. _____

2. _____   5. _____   8. _____

3. _____   6. _____   9. _____

10. _____   11. _____   12. _____

Third Species:

Counterpoint Assignment, no. 3

Name _____

Examine the following excerpt. Locate at least 12 errors in voice leading, melodic writing or harmonic structure. Circle each and indicate each by type and measure number in the spaces provided below. Then compose an alternative Third Species counterpoints to the *cantus firmus*, on the staff above. Analyze the counterpoint between your new melody and the *cantus firmus*, showing all the harmonic intervals between the two highest staves. Identify embellishing tones, like Consonant Passing tones (CP), Dissonant Passing tones (DP), Consonant Neighbor tones (CN), etc. by labeling each accordingly above the note.

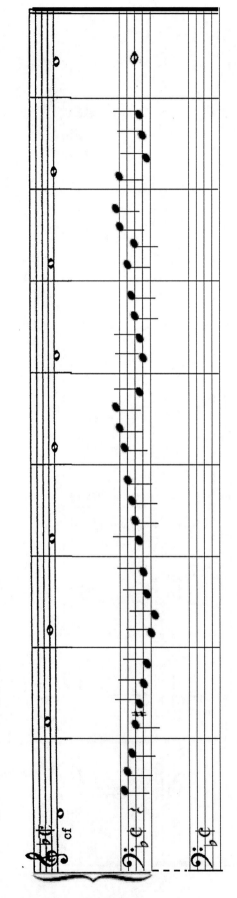

1. _____
2. _____
3. _____
10. _____

4. _____
5. _____
6. _____
11. _____

7. _____
8. _____
9. _____
12. _____

Third Species:

Counterpoint Assignment, no. 4

Name _____

Analyze the following excerpt, indicating each harmonic interval between the staves and identifying embellishing tones like Dissonant Passing tones (DP), Consonant Passing tones (CP), Dissonant Neighbor tones, Consonant Neighbor tones (CN) Double Neighbors (DN) and *Nota Cambiatas* (NC) in the appropriate manner. Then compose two alternative Third Species counterpoints to the *cantus firmus*, one above and one below. Analyze the counterpoint with each in the same way.

Third Species:

Counterpoint Assignment, no. 5

Name _____

Analyze the following excerpt, indicating each harmonic interval between the staves and identifying embellishing tones like Dissonant Passing tones (DP), Consonant Passing tones (CP), Dissonant Neighbor tones, Consonant Neighbor tones (CN) Double Neighbors (DN) and *Nota Cambiatas* (NC) in the appropriate manner. Then compose two alternative Third Species counterpoints to the *cantus firmus*, one above and one below. Analyze the counterpoint with each in the same way.

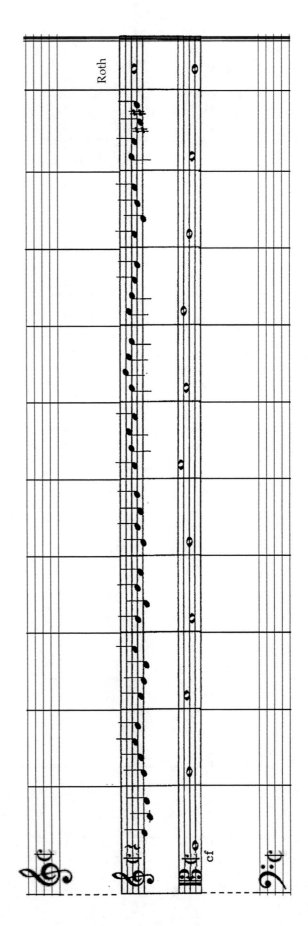

Third Species:

Counterpoint Assignment, no. 6

Name _____

Analyze the following excerpt, indicating each harmonic interval between the staves and identifying embellishing tones like Dissonant Passing tones (DP), Consonant Passing tones (CP), Dissonant Neighbor tones, Consonant Neighbor tones (CN) Double Neighbors (DN) and *Nota Cambiatas* (NC) in the appropriate manner. Then compose two alternative Third Species counterpoints to the *cantus firmus*, one above and one below. Analyze the counterpoint with each in the same way.

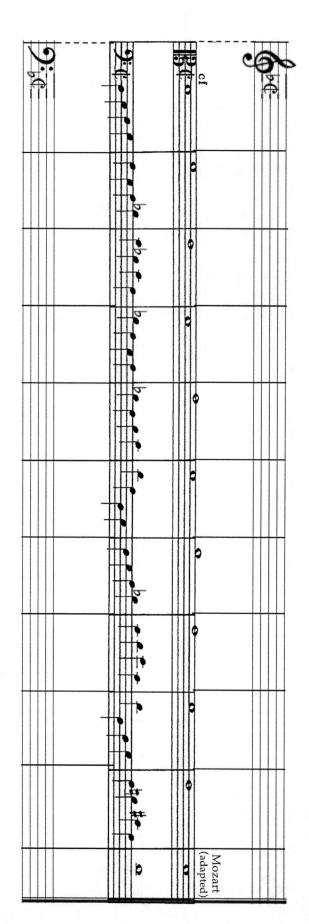

Mozart
(adapted)

Third Species:

Counterpoint Assignment, no. 7

Name _____

Analyze the following excerpt, indicating each harmonic interval between the staves and identifying embellishing tones like Dissonant Passing tones (DP), Consonant Passing tones (CP), Dissonant Neighbor tones, Consonant Neighbor tones (CN) Double Neighbors (DN) and *Nota Cambiatas* (NC) in the appropriate manner. Then compose two alternative Third Species counterpoints to the *cantus firmus*, one above and one below. Analyze the counterpoint with each in the same way.

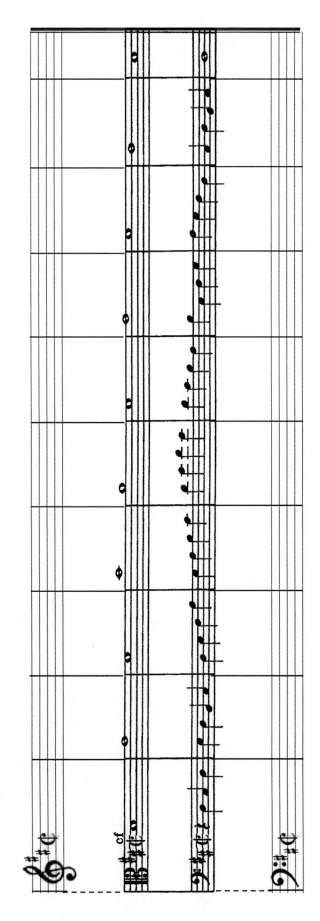

Third Species:

Counterpoint Assignment, no. 8

Name _____

Compose two Third-Species counterpoints to the given *cantus firmus*, one above and one below. Refer to Units 1, 2, 3 and 4 of the *Introduction to Two-Part Species Counterpoint* (pp. 1-16) and the examples discussed in class as models. Analyze the passages, showing all harmonic intervals as we did in class. Identify all Consonant Passing tones (CP), Dissonant Passing tones (DP) Consonant Neighbor tones (CN) etc., with appropriate abbreviations.

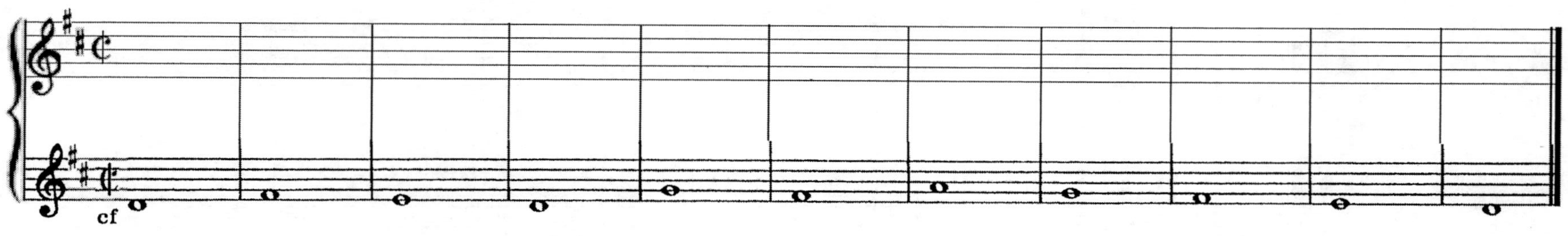

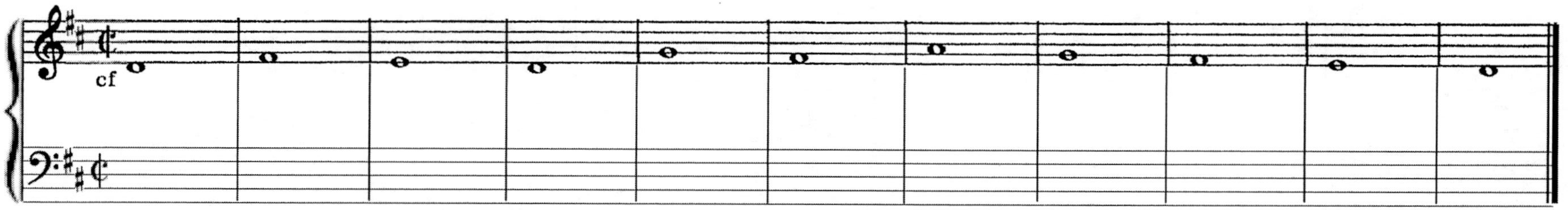

Third Species:

Counterpoint Assignment, no. 9

Name _____

Compose two Third-Species counterpoints to the given *cantus firmus*, one above and one below. Refer to Units 1, 2, 3 and 4 of the *Introduction to Two-Part Species Counterpoint* (pp. 1-16) and the examples discussed in class as models. Analyze the passages, showing all harmonic intervals as we did in class. Identify all Consonant Passing tones (CP), Dissonant Passing tones (DP), Consonant Neighbor tones (CN), etc., with appropriate abbreviations.

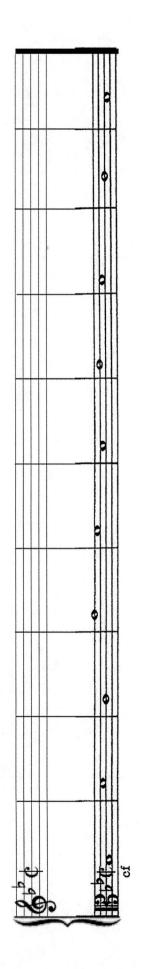

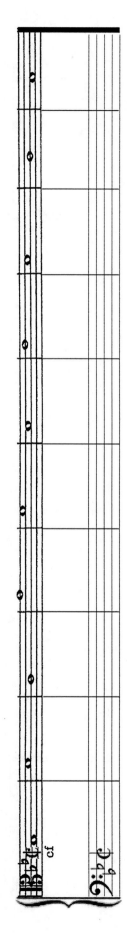

Third Species:

Counterpoint Assignment, no. 10

Name _____

Compose two Third-Species counterpoints to the given *cantus firmus*, one above and one below. Refer to Units 1, 2, 3 and 4 of the *Introduction to Two-Part Species Counterpoint* (pp. 1-16) and the examples discussed in class as models. Analyze the passages, showing all harmonic intervals as we did in class. Identify all Consonant Passing tones (CP), Dissonant Passing tones (DP), Consonant Neighbor tones (CN), etc., with appropriate abbreviations.

Counterpoint Assignment, no. 11

Name _____

Third Species:

Compose two Third-Species counterpoints to the given *cantus firmus*, one above and one below. Refer to Units 1, 2, 3 and 4 of the *Introduction to Two-Part Species Counterpoint* (pp. 1-16) and the examples discussed in class as models. Analyze the passages, showing all harmonic intervals as we did in class. Identify all Consonant Passing tones (CP), Dissonant Passing tones (DP), Consonant Neighbor tones (CN), etc., with appropriate abbreviations.

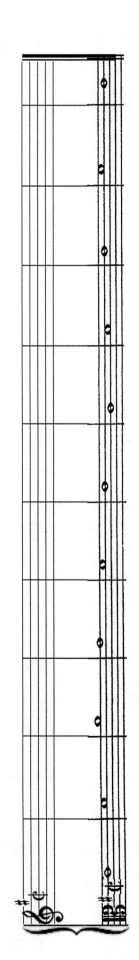

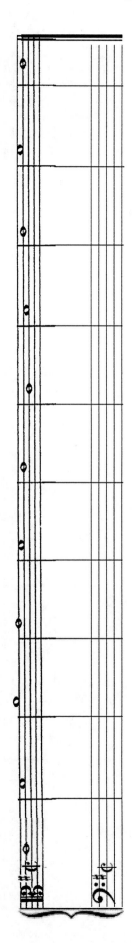

Third Species:

Counterpoint Assignment, no. 12

Name _____

Compose three counterpoints above the given *cantus firmus*, one in First Species, one in Second Species and one in Third Species. Compose the first species example first; then base the second species example upon it and the third species example upon the second species one. Refer to Units 1, 2, 3 and 4 of the *Introduction to Two-Part Species Counterpoint* (pp. 1–16) and the examples discussed in class as models. Analyze the passages, showing all harmonic intervals between each counterpoint and the CF below that counterpoint as we did in class. Identify all passing tones, neighbor tones and other figuration patterns with appropriate abbreviations.

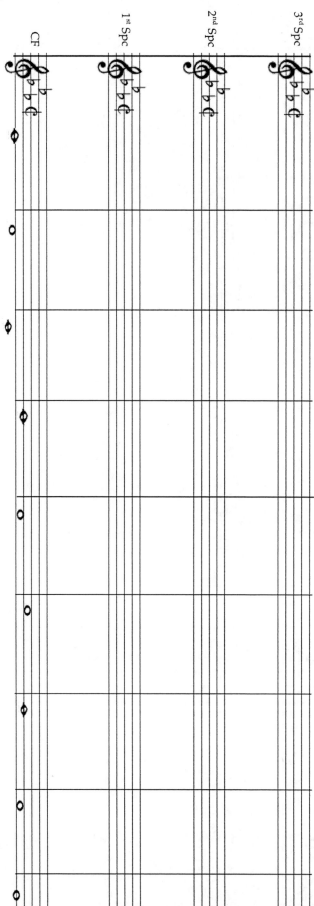

Counterpoint Assignment, no. 13

Name _____

Third Species:

Compose three counterpoints above the given *cantus firmus*, one in First Species, one in Second Species and one in Third Species. Compose the first species example first; then base the second species example upon it and the third species example upon the second species one. Refer to Units 1, 2, 3 and 4 of the *Introduction to Two-Part Species Counterpoint* (pp. 1-16) and the examples discussed in class as models. Analyze the passages, showing all harmonic intervals between each counterpoint and the CF below that counterpoint as we did in class. Identify all passing tones, neighbor tones and other figuration patterns with appropriate abbreviations.

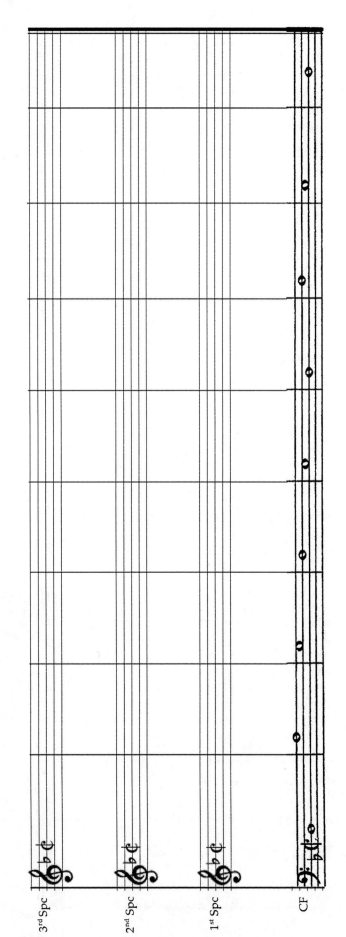

Third Species:

Counterpoint Assignment, no. 14

Name _____

Compose three counterpoints below the given *cantus firmus*, one in First Species, one in Second Species and one in Third Species. Compose the first species example first; then base the second species example upon it and the third species example upon the second species one. Refer to Units 1, 2, 3 and 4 of the *Introduction to Two-Part Species Counterpoint* (pp. 1-16) and the examples discussed in class as models. Analyze the passages, showing all harmonic intervals between each counterpoint and the CF below that counterpoint as we did in class. Identify all passing tones, neighbor tones and other figuration patterns with appropriate abbreviations.

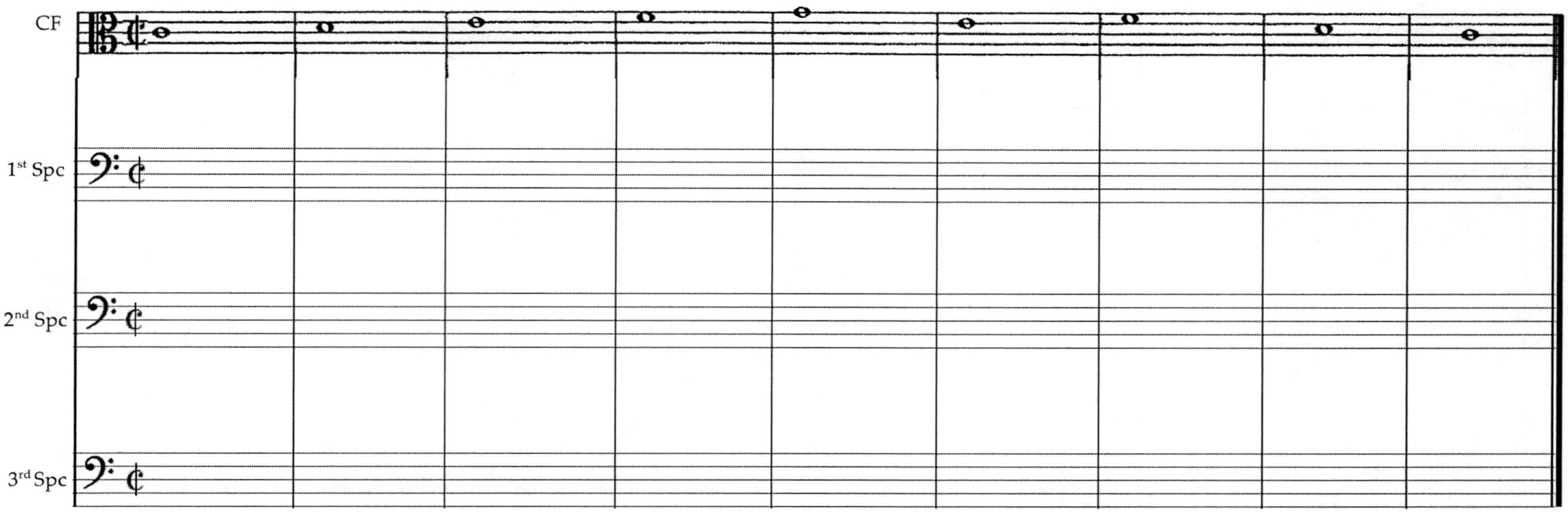

Third Species:

Counterpoint Assignment, no. 15

Name _____

Compose three counterpoints below the given *cantus firmus*, one in First Species, one in Second Species and one in Third Species. Compose the first species example first; then base the second species example upon it and the third species example upon the second species one. Refer to Units 1, 2, 3 and 4 of the *Introduction to Two-Part Species Counterpoint* (pp. 1-16) and the examples discussed in class as models. Analyze the passages, showing all harmonic intervals between each counterpoint and the CF below that counterpoint as we did in class. Identify all passing tones, neighbor tones and other figuration patterns with appropriate abbreviations.

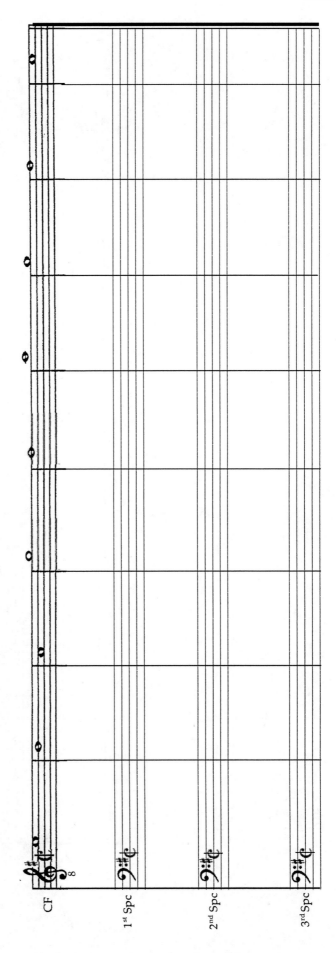

Fourth Species:

Counterpoint Assignment, no. 1

Name

Examine the following excerpt. Locate at least 10 errors in voice leading, melodic writing or harmonic structure. Circle each and indicate each by type and measure number in the spaces provided below. Then compose an alternative Fourth Species counterpoints to the *cantus firmus*, on the staff above. Analyze the counterpoint between your new melody and the *cantus firmus*, identifying embellishing tones like Suspensions (Sus), Syncopations (Syn), etc. by labeling each accordingly above the note. Identify examples of "Broken Species" (BR) as well.

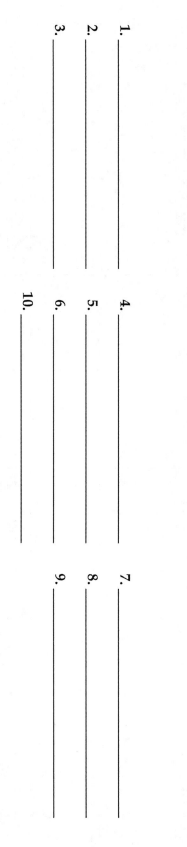

1. _____

2. _____

3. _____

4. _____

5. _____

6. _____

7. _____

8. _____

9. _____

10. _____

Fourth Species:

Counterpoint Assignment, no. 2

Name _____

Examine the following excerpt. Locate at least 8 errors in voice leading, melodic writing or harmonic structure. Circle each and indicate each by type and measure number in the spaces provided below. Then compose an alternative Fourth Species counterpoints to the *cantus firmus*, on the staff below. Analyze the counterpoint between your new melody and the *cantus firmus*, identifying embellishing tones like Suspensions (Sus), Syncopations (Syn), etc. by labeling each accordingly above the note. Identify examples of "Broken Species" (BR) as well.

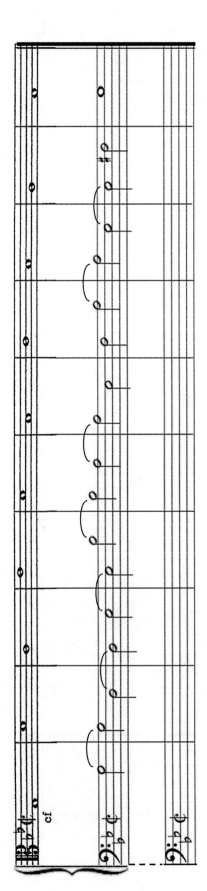

1. _____

2. _____

3. _____

4. _____

5. _____

6. _____

7. _____

8. _____

Fourth Species:

Counterpoint Assignment, no. 3

Name _____

Examine the following excerpt. Locate at least 8 errors in voice leading, melodic writing or harmonic structure. Circle each and indicate each by type and measure number in the spaces provided below. Then compose an alternative Fourth Species counterpoints to the *cantus firmus*, on the staff above. Analyze the counterpoint between your new melody and the *cantus firmus*, identifying embellishing tones like Suspensions (Sus), Syncopations (Syn), etc. by labeling each according above the note. Identify examples of "Broken Species" (BR) as well.

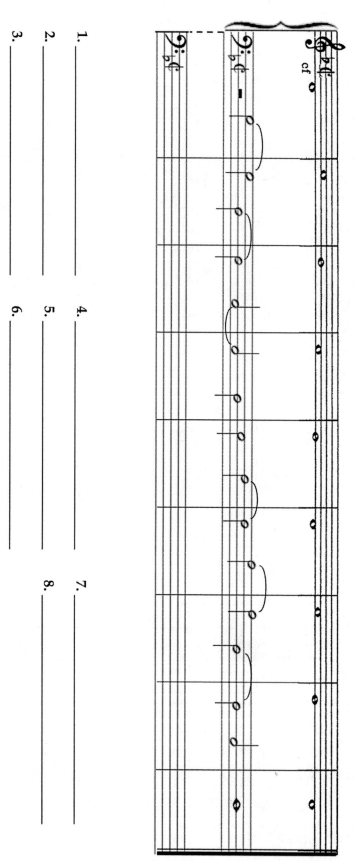

1. _____

2. _____

3. _____

4. _____

5. _____

6. _____

7. _____

8. _____

Fourth Species:

Counterpoint Assignment, no. 4

Name _____

Analyze the following excerpt, indicating each harmonic interval between the staves and identifying embellishing tones like Suspensions (Sus), Syncopations (Syn), etc. in the appropriate manner. Identify examples of "Broken Species" (BR) as well. Then compose two alternative Fourth Species counterpoints to the *cantus firmus*, one above and one below. Analyze the counterpoint with each in the same way.

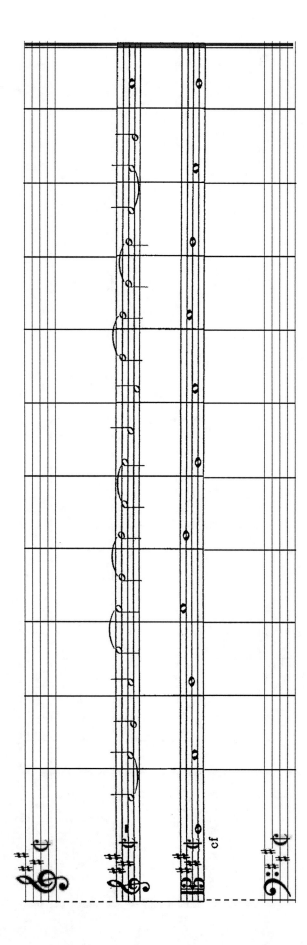

Fourth Species:

Counterpoint Assignment, no. 5

Name _____

Analyze the following excerpt, indicating each harmonic interval between the staves and identifying embellishing tones like Suspensions (Sus), Syncopations (Syn), etc. in the appropriate manner. Identify examples of "Broken Species" (BR) as well. Then compose two alternative Fourth Species counterpoints to the *cantus firmus*, one above and one below. Analyze the counterpoint with each in the same way.

Fourth Species:

Counterpoint Assignment, no. 6

Name _____

Analyze the following excerpt, indicating each harmonic interval between the staves and identifying embellishing tones like Suspensions (Sus), Syncopations (Syn), etc. in the appropriate manner. Identify examples of "Broken Species" (BR) as well. Then compose two alternative Fourth Species counterpoints to the *cantus firmus*, one above and one below. Analyze the counterpoint with each in the same way.

Fourth Species:

Counterpoint Assignment, no. 7

Name _____

Analyze the following excerpt, indicating each harmonic interval between the staves and identifying embellishing tones like Suspensions (Sus), Syncopations (Syn), etc. in the appropriate manner. Identify examples of "Broken Species" (BR) as well. Then compose two alternative Fourth Species counterpoints to the *cantus firmus*, one above and one below. Analyze the counterpoint with each in the same way.

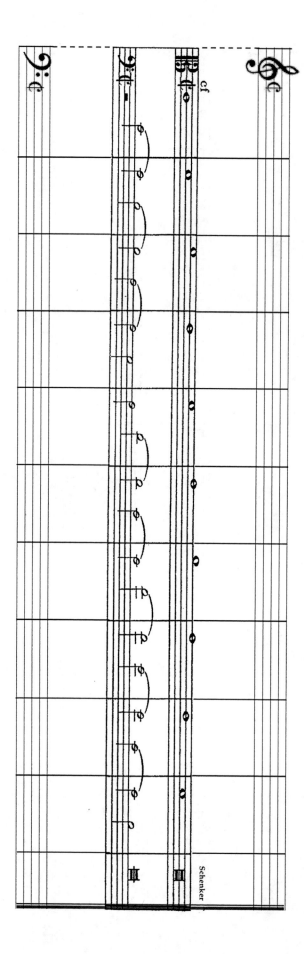

Fourth Species:

Counterpoint Assignment, no. 8

Name _____

Compose two Fourth-Species counterpoints to the given *cantus firmus,* one above and one below. Refer to Units 1-5 of the *Introduction to Two-Part Species Counterpoint* (pp. 1-28) and the examples discussed in class as models. Analyze the passages, showing all harmonic intervals as we did in class by showing the harmonic intervals below the staves and identifying all embellishing tones like Suspensions (Sus), Syncopations (Syn), etc., in the appropriate manner. Identify examples of Broken Species (BR) as well.

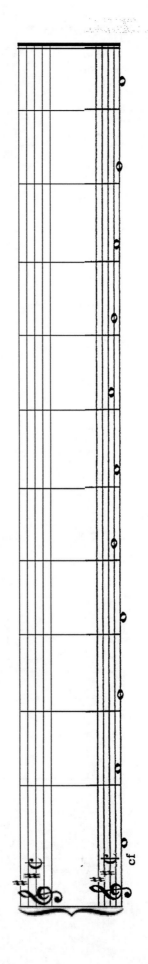

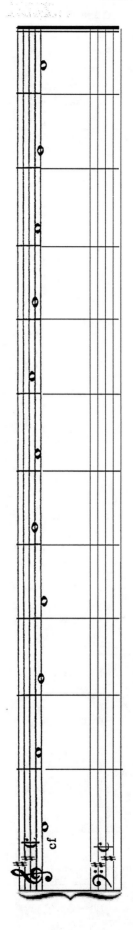

Fourth Species:

Counterpoint Assignment, no. 9

Name _____

Compose two Fourth-Species counterpoints to the given *cantus firmus*, one above and one below. Refer to Units 1-5 of the *Introduction to Two-Part Species Counterpoint* (pp. 1-28) and the examples discussed in class as models. Analyze the passages, showing all harmonic intervals as we did in class by indicating each harmonic interval below the staves and identifying all embellishing tones like Suspensions (Sus), Syncopations (Syn), etc., in the appropriate manner. Identify examples of "Broken Species" (BR) as well.

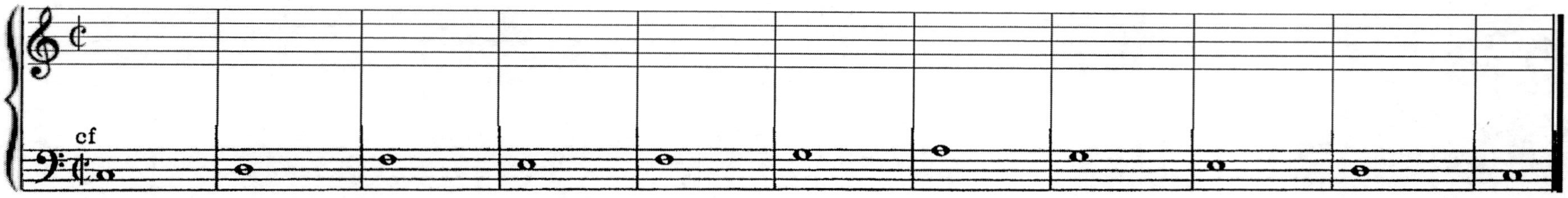

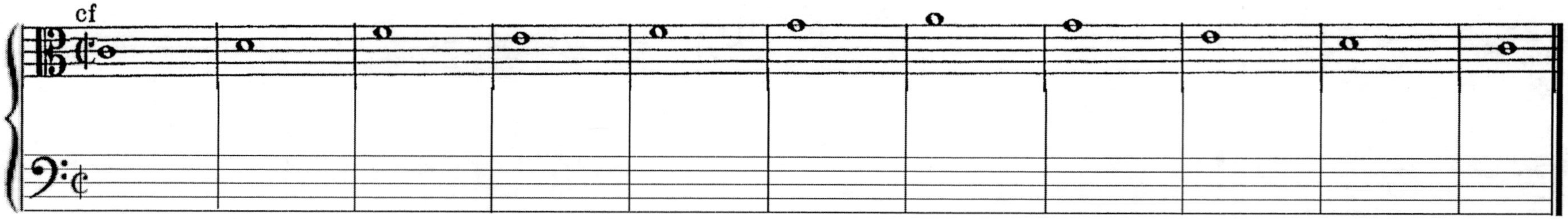

Fourth Species:

Counterpoint Assignment, no. 10

Name _____

Compose two Fourth-Species counterpoints to the given *cantus firmus*, one above and one below. Refer to Units 1-5 of the *Introduction to Two-Part Species Counterpoint* (pp. 1-28) and the examples discussed in class as models. Analyze the passages, showing all harmonic intervals as we did in class by indicating each harmonic interval below the staves and identifying all embellishing tones like Suspensions (Sus), Syncopations (Syn), etc., in the appropriate manner. Identify examples of "Broken Species" (BR) as well.

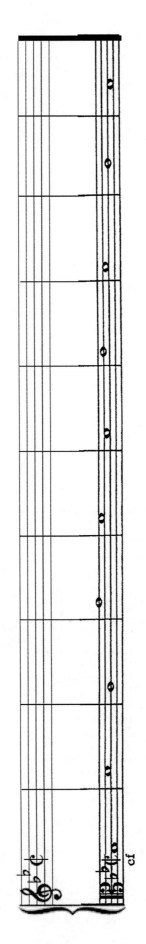

Fourth Species:

Counterpoint Assignment, no. 11

Name _____

Compose two Fourth-Species counterpoints to the given *cantus firmus*, one above and one below. Refer to Units 1-5 of the *Introduction to Two-Part Species Counterpoint* (pp. 1-28) and the examples discussed in class as models. Analyze the passages, showing all harmonic intervals as we did in class by indicting each harmonic interval below the staves and identifying embellishing tones like Suspensions (Sus), Syncopations (Syn), etc. in the appropriate manner. Identify examples of "Broken Species" (BR) as well.

Fourth Species:

Counterpoint Assignment, no. 12

Name _____

Compose three counterpoints below the given *cantus firmus*, one in First Species, one in Second Species and one in Fourth Species. Compose the FOURTH species example first; then base the FIRST species example upon it and the SECOND species example upon the FIRST species one. Refer to Units 1-5 of the *Introduction to Two-Part Species Counterpoint* (pp. 1-27) and the examples discussed in class as models. Analyze the passages, showing all harmonic intervals between each counterpoint and the CF below that counterpoint as we did in class. Identify all suspensions, syncopations, passing tones, neighbor tones and other figuration patterns with appropriate abbreviations.

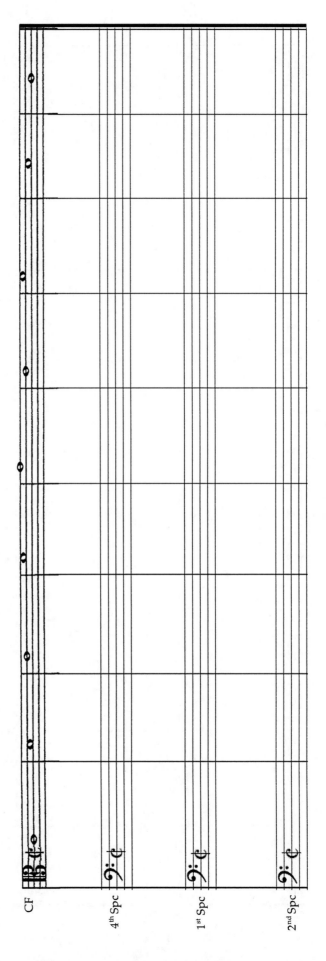

CF

4th Spc

1st Spc

2nd Spc

Fourth Species:

Counterpoint Assignment, no. 13

Name _____

Compose three counterpoints above the given *cantus firmus*, one in First Species, one in Second Species and one in Fourth Species. Compose the FOURTH species example first; then base the FIRST species example upon it and the SECOND species example upon the FIRST species one. Refer to Units 1-5 of the *Introduction to Two-Part Species Counterpoint* (pp. 1-27) and the examples discussed in class as models. Analyze the passages, showing all harmonic intervals between each counterpoint and the CF below that counterpoint as we did in class. Identify all suspensions, syncopations, passing tones, neighbor tones and other figuration patterns with appropriate abbreviations.

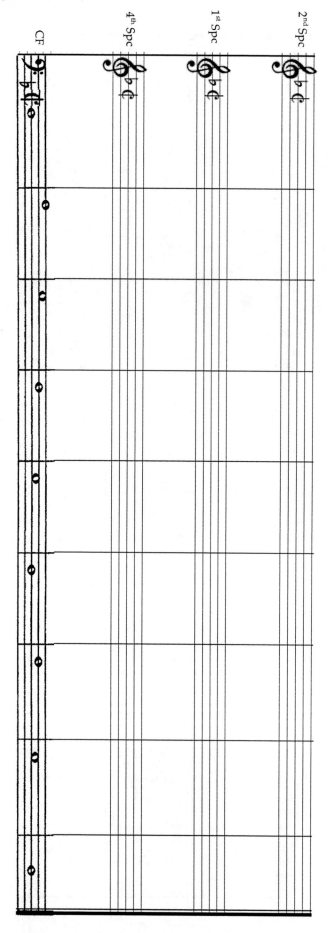

Fourth Species:

Counterpoint Assignment, no. 14

Name _____

Compose three counterpoints above the given *cantus firmus*, one in First Species, one in Second Species and one in Fourth Species. Compose the FOURTH species example first; then base the FIRST species example upon it and the SECOND species example upon the FIRST species one. Refer to Units 1-5 of the *Introduction to Two-Part Species Counterpoint* (pp. 1-27) and the examples discussed in class as models. Analyze the passages, showing all harmonic intervals between each counterpoint and the CF below that counterpoint as we did in class. Identify all suspensions, syncopations, passing tones, neighbor tones and other figuration patterns with appropriate abbreviations.

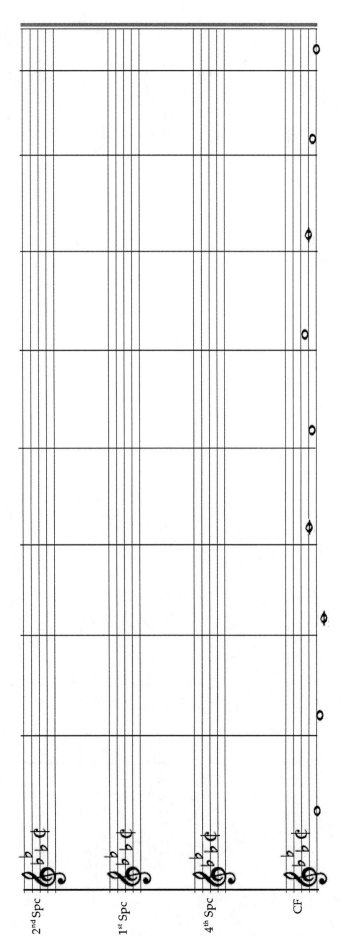

Fifth Species:

Counterpoint Assignment, no. 1

Name _____

Examine the following excerpt. Locate at least 12 errors in voice leading, melodic writing or harmonic structure. Circle each and indicate each by type and measure number in the spaces provided below. Then compose an alternative Fifth Species counterpoints to the *cantus firmus*, on the staff above. Analyze the counterpoint between your new melody and the *cantus firmus*, identifying embellishing tones like Passing tones (P), Neighbor tones (N), Suspensions (Sus), Syncopations (Syn), etc. by labeling each according above the note.

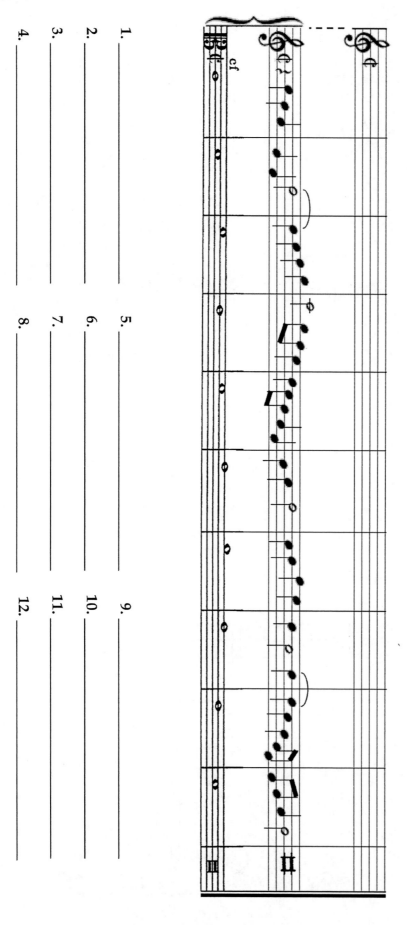

1. _____
2. _____
3. _____
4. _____
5. _____
6. _____
7. _____
8. _____
9. _____
10. _____
11. _____
12. _____

Fifth Species:

Counterpoint Assignment, no. 2

Name _____

Examine the following excerpt. Locate at least 12 errors in voice leading, melodic writing or harmonic structure. Circle each and indicate each by type and measure number in the spaces provided below. Then compose an alternative Fifth Species counterpoints to the *cantus firmus,* on the staff above. Analyze the counterpoint between your new melody and the *cantus firmus,* identifying embellishing tones like Passing tones (P), Neighbor tones (N), Suspensions (Sus), Syncopations (Syn), etc. by labeling each accordingly above the note.

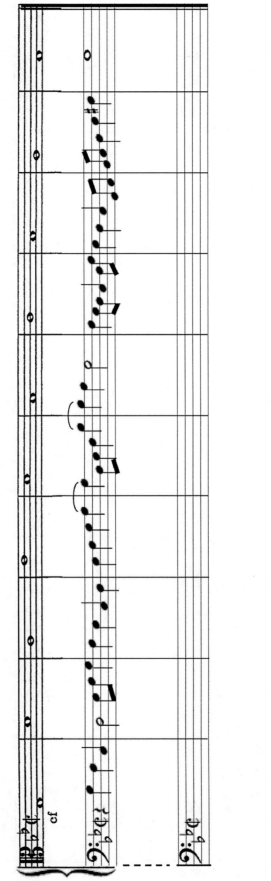
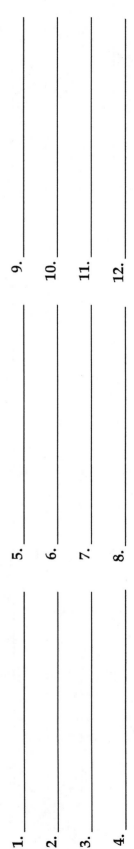

1. _____

2. _____

3. _____

4. _____

5. _____

6. _____

7. _____

8. _____

9. _____

10. _____

11. _____

12. _____

Fifth Species:

Counterpoint Assignment, no. 3

Name

Examine the following excerpt. Locate at least 12 errors in voice leading, melodic writing or harmonic structure. Circle each and indicate each by type and measure number in the spaces provided below. Then compose an alternative Fifth Species counterpoints to the *cantus firmus*, on the staff above. Analyze the counterpoint between your new melody and the *cantus firmus*, identifying embellishing tones like Passing tones (P), Neighbor tones (N), Suspensions (Sus), Syncopations (Syn), etc. by labeling each accordingly above the note.

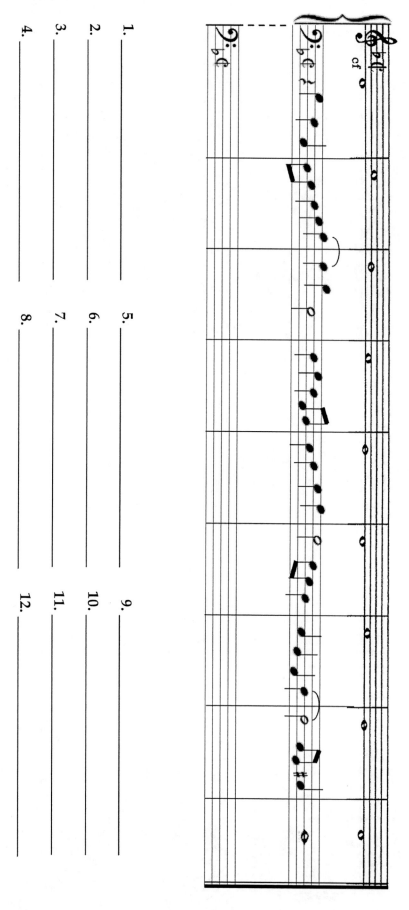

1. _____

2. _____

3. _____

4. _____

5. _____

6. _____

7. _____

8. _____

9. _____

10. _____

11. _____

12. _____

Fifth Species:

Counterpoint Assignment, no. 4

Name _____

Analyze the following excerpt, indicating each harmonic interval between the staves and identifying embellishing tones like Consonant Passing, (CP), Dissonant Passing (DP), Consonant Neighbors (CN), Dissonant Neighbors (DN), Double Neighbors (DN), *Nota Cambiatus* (NC), Suspensions (Sus), Syncopations (Syn), Decorate Resolutions (DR), etc. in the appropriate manner. Then compose two alternative Fifth Species counterpoints to the *cantus firmus*, one above and one below. Analyze the counterpoint with each in the same way.

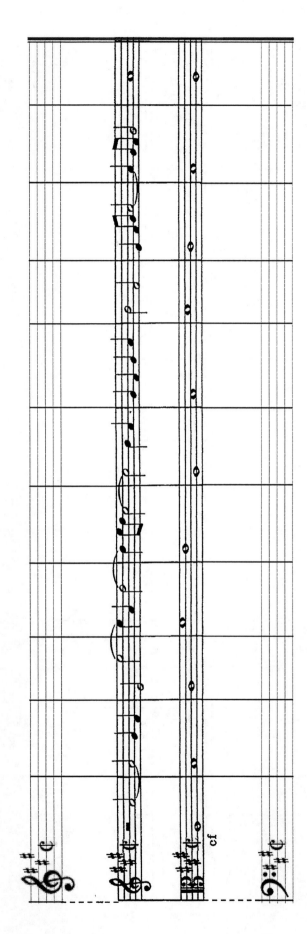

Fifth Species:

Counterpoint Assignment, no. 5

Name _____

Analyze the following excerpt, indicating each harmonic interval between the staves and identifying embellishing tones like Consonant Passing, (CP), Dissonant Passing (DP), Consonant Neighbors (CN), Dissonant Neighbors (DN), Double Neighbors (DN), *Nota Cambiatas* (NC), Suspensions (Sus), Syncopations (Syn), Decorate Resolutions (DR), etc. in the appropriate manner. Then compose two alternative Fifth Species counterpoints to the *cantus firmus*, one above and one below. Analyze the counterpoint with each in the same way.

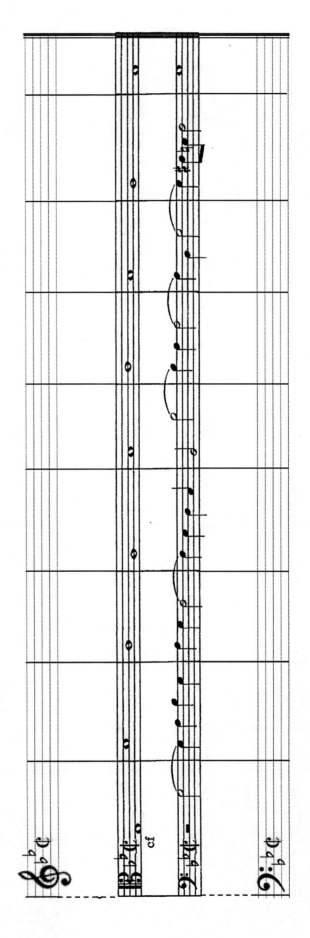

Fifth Species:

Counterpoint Assignment, no. 6

Name _____

Analyze the following excerpt, indicating each harmonic interval between the staves and identifying embellishing tones like Consonant Passing, (CP), Dissonant Passing (DP), Consonant Neighbors (CN), Dissonant Neighbors (DN), Double Neighbors (DN), *Nota Cambiatas* (NC), Suspensions (Sus), Syncopations (Syn), Decorate Resolutions (DR), etc. in the appropriate manner. Then compose two alternative Fifth Species counterpoints to the *cantus firmus*, one above and one below. Analyze the counterpoint with each in the same way.

Fifth Species:

Counterpoint Assignment, no. 7

Name _____

Analyze the following excerpt, indicating each harmonic interval between the staves and identifying embellishing tones like Consonant Passing, (CP), Dissonant Passing (DP), Consonant Neighbors (CN), Dissonant Neighbors (DN), Double Neighbors (DN), *Nota Cambiatas* (NC), Suspensions (Sus), Syncopations (Syn), Decorate Resolutions (DR), etc. in the appropriate manner. Then compose two alternative Fifth Species counterpoints to the *cantus firmus*, one above and one below. Analyze the counterpoint with each in the same way.

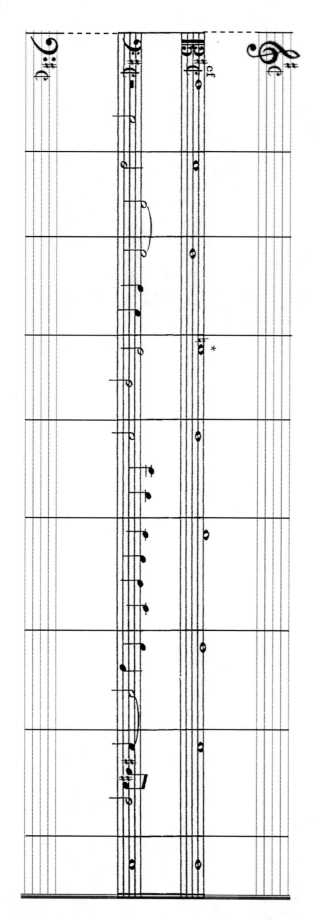

* Why is it F♮ here, even though it is not in the key? What melodic error is it intended to avoid?

Fifth Species:

Counterpoint Assignment, no. 8

Name _____

Compose two Fifth-Species counterpoints to the given *cantus firmus*, one above and one below. Refer to Units 1-6 of the *Introduction to Two-Part Species Counterpoint* (pp. 1-41) and the examples discussed in class as models. Analyze the passages, showing all harmonic intervals as we did in class. Identify all Passing tones (P), Neighbor tones (N), Suspensions (Sus) etc., with appropriate abbreviations.

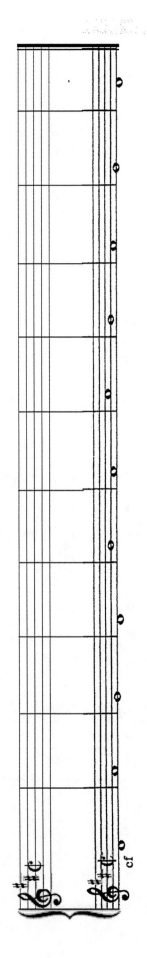

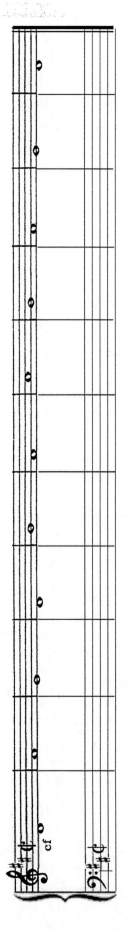

Fifth Species:

Counterpoint Assignment, no. 9

Name _____

Compose two Fifth-Species counterpoints to the given *cantus firmus*, one above and one below. Refer to Units 1-6 of the *Introduction to Two-Part Species Counterpoint* (pp. 1-41) and the examples discussed in class as models. Analyze the passages, showing all harmonic intervals as we did in class. Identify all Passing tones (P), Neighbor tones (N), Suspensions (Sus) etc., with appropriate abbreviations.

Counterpoint Assignment, no. 10

Name _____

Fifth Species:

Compose two Fifth-Species counterpoints to the given *cantus firmus*, one above and one below. Refer to Units 1-6 of the *Introduction to Two-Part Species Counterpoint* (pp. 1-41) and the examples discussed in class as models. Analyze the passages, showing all harmonic intervals as we did in class. Identify all Passing tones (CP), Neighbor tones (N), Suspensions (Sus) etc., with appropriate abbreviations.

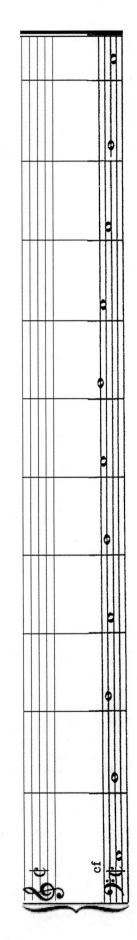

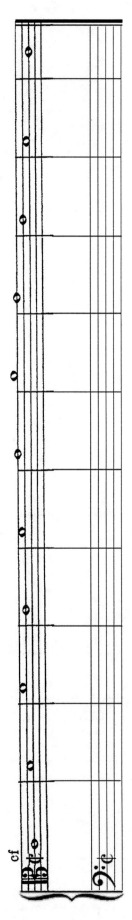

Fifth Species:

Counterpoint Assignment, no. 11

Name _____

Compose two Fifth-Species counterpoints to the given *cantus firmus*, one above and one below. Refer to Units 1-6 of the *Introduction to Two-Part Species Counterpoint* (pp. 1-41) and the examples discussed in class as models. Analyze the passages, showing all harmonic intervals as we did in class. Identify all Passing tones (CP), Neighbor tones (N), Suspensions (Sus) etc., with appropriate abbreviations.

Fifth Species:

Counterpoint Assignment, no. 12

Name _____

Compose three counterpoints below the given *cantus firmus*, one in First Species, one in Second Species and one in Fifth Species. Compose the FIFTH species example first; then base the SECOND species example upon it and the FIRST species example upon the SECOND species one. Refer to Units 1-6 of the *Introduction to Two-Part Species Counterpoint* (pp. 1-41) and the examples discussed in class as models. Analyze the passages, showing all harmonic intervals between each counterpoint and the CF below that counterpoint as we did in class. Identify all suspensions, syncopations, passing tones, neighbor tones and other figuration patterns with appropriate abbreviations.

CF

5th Spc

2nd Spc

1st Spc

Fifth Species:

Counterpoint Assignment, no. 13

Name _____

Compose three counterpoints above the given *cantus firmus*, one in First Species, one in Second Species and one in Fifth Species. Compose the FIFTH species example first; then base the SECOND species example upon it and the FIRST species example upon the SECOND species example one. Refer to Units 1-6 of the *Introduction to Two-Part Species Counterpoint* (pp. 1-39) and the examples discussed in class as models. Analyze the passages, showing all harmonic intervals between each counterpoint and the CF below that counterpoint as we did in class. Identify all suspensions, syncopations, passing tones, neighbor tones and other figuration patterns with appropriate abbreviations.

Fifth Species:

Counterpoint Assignment, no. 14

Name _____

Compose three counterpoints above the given *cantus firmus*, one in First Species, one in Second Species and one in Fifth Species. Compose the FIFTH species example first; then base the SECOND species example upon it and the FIRST species example upon the SECOND species one. Refer to Units 1-6 of the *Introduction to Two-Part Species Counterpoint* (pp. 1-41) and the examples discussed in class as models. Analyze the passages, showing all harmonic intervals between each counterpoint and the CF below that counterpoint as we did in class. Identify all suspensions, syncopations, passing tones, neighbor tones and other figuration patterns with appropriate abbreviations.

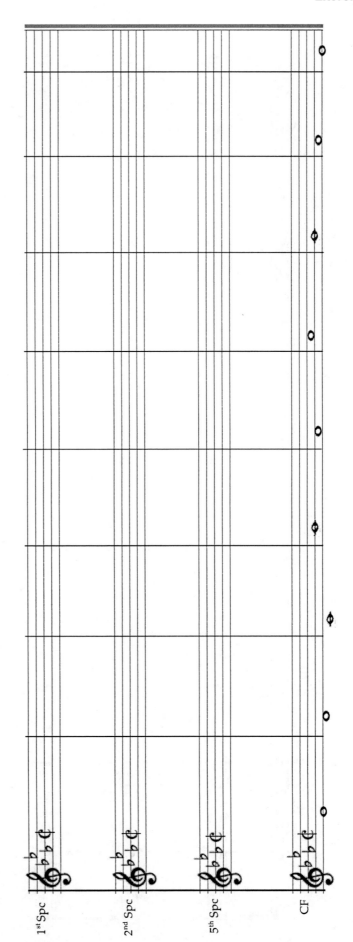

Fifth Species:

Counterpoint Assignment, no. 15

Name _____

Analyze the following excerpt, indicating each harmonic interval between the staves and identifying embellishing tones like Consonant Passing, (CP), Dissonant Passing (DP), Consonant Neighbors (CN), Dissonant Neighbors (DN), Double Neighbors (DN), *Nota Cambiatas* (NC), Suspensions (Sus), Syncopations (Syn), Decorate Resolutions (DR), etc. in the appropriate manner. Then compose two alternative counterpoints above the given *cantus firmus* that could represent simplifications of the given Fifth Species example, one in Fourth Species and one in First Species. Analyze the counterpoint between the *cantus firmus* and these counterpoints in the same way

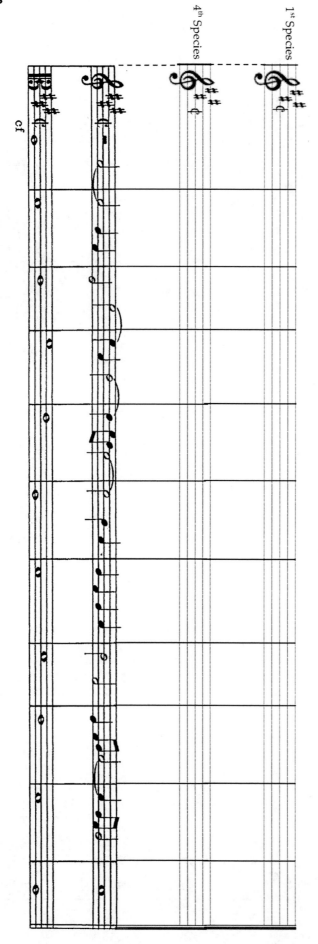

Fifth Species:

Analyze the following excerpt, indicating each harmonic interval between the staves and identifying embellishing tones like Consonant Passing, (CP), Dissonant Passing (DP), Consonant Neighbors (CN), Dissonant Neighbors (DN), Double Neighbors (DN), *Nota Cambiatas* (NC), Suspensions (Sus), Syncopations (Syn), Decorate Resolutions (DR), etc. in the appropriate manner. Then compose two alternative counterpoints above the given *cantus firmus* that could represent simplifications of the given Fifth Species example, one in Fourth Species and one in First Species. Analyze the counterpoint between the *cantus firmus* and these counterpoints in the same way

Counterpoint Assignment, no. 16

Name _____

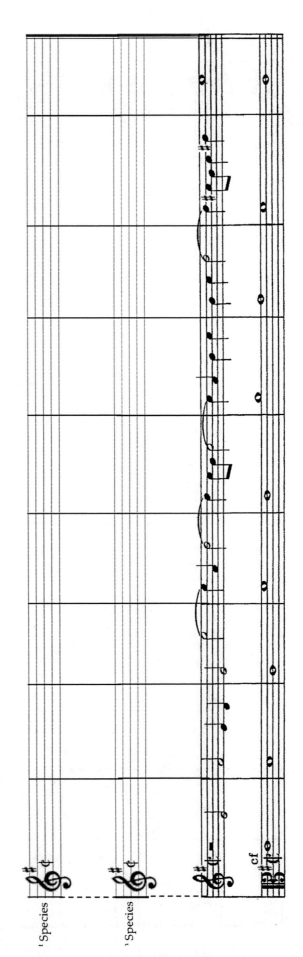

Fifth Species:

Counterpoint Assignment, no. 17

Name _____

Analyze the following excerpt, indicating each harmonic interval between the staves and identifying embellishing tones like Consonant Passing, (CP), Dissonant Passing (DP), Consonant Neighbors (CN), Dissonant Neighbors (DN), Double Neighbors (DN), *Nota Cambiatas* (NC), Suspensions (Sus), Syncopations (Syn), Decorate Resolutions (DR), etc. in the appropriate manner. Then compose two alternative counterpoints above the given *cantus firmus* that could represent simplifications of the given Fifth Species example, one in Second Species and one in First Species. Analyze the counterpoint between the *cantus firmus* and these counterpoints in the same way

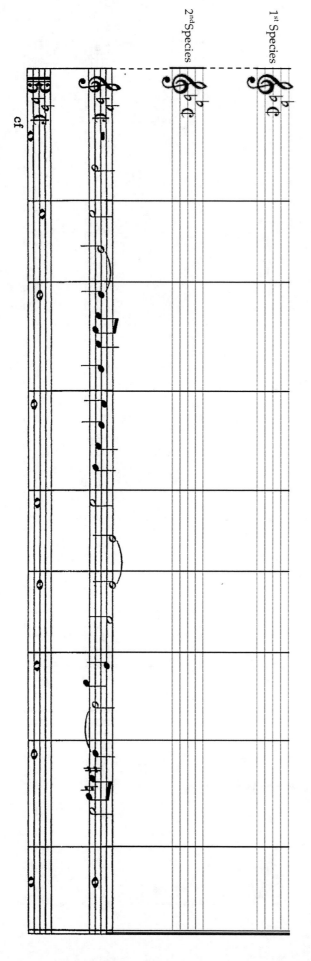

Fifth Species:

Counterpoint Assignment, no. 18

Name _____

Analyze the following excerpt, indicating each harmonic interval between the staves and identifying embellishing tones like Consonant Passing, (CP), Dissonant Passing (DP), Consonant Neighbors (CN), Dissonant Neighbors (DN), Double Neighbors (DN), *Nota Cambiatas* (NC), Suspensions (Sus), Syncopations (Syn), Decorate Resolutions (DR), etc. in the appropriate manner. Then compose two alternative counterpoints above the given *cantus firmus* that could represent simplifications of the given Fifth Species example, one in Second Species and one in First Species. Analyze the counterpoint between the *cantus firmus* and these counterpoints in the same way

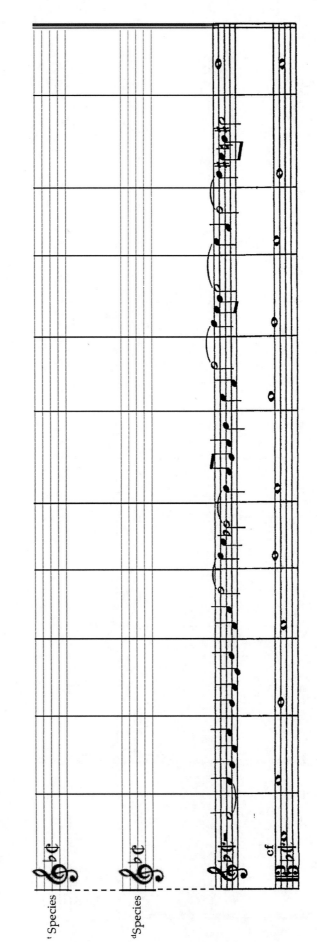

Fifth Species:

Counterpoint Assignment, no. 19

Name _____

Analyze the following excerpt, indicating each harmonic interval between the staves and identifying embellishing tones like Consonant Passing, (CP), Dissonant Passing (DP), Consonant Neighbors (CN), Dissonant Neighbors (DN), Double Neighbors (DN), *Nota Cambiatas* (NC), Suspensions (Sus), Syncopations (Syn), Decorate Resolutions (DR), etc. in the appropriate manner. Then compose two alternative counterpoints above the given *cantus firmus* that could represent simplifications of the given Fifth Species example, one in Fourth Species and one in First Species. Analyze the counterpoint between the *cantus firmus* and these counterpoints in the same way

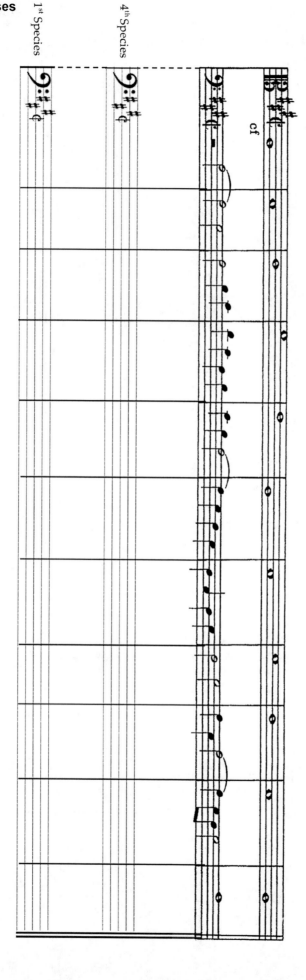

Counterpoint Assignment, no. 20

Name _____

Fifth Species:

Analyze the following excerpt, indicating each harmonic interval between the staves and identifying embellishing tones like Consonant Passing, (CP), Dissonant Passing (DP), Consonant Neighbors (CN), Dissonant Neighbors (DN), Double Neighbors (DN), *Nota Cambiatas* (NC), Suspensions (Sus), Syncopations (Syn), Decorate Resolutions (DR), etc. in the appropriate manner. Then compose two alternative counterpoints above the given *cantus firmus* that could represent simplifications of the given Fifth Species example, one in Second Species and one in First Species. Analyze the counterpoint between the *cantus firmus* and these counterpoints in the same way

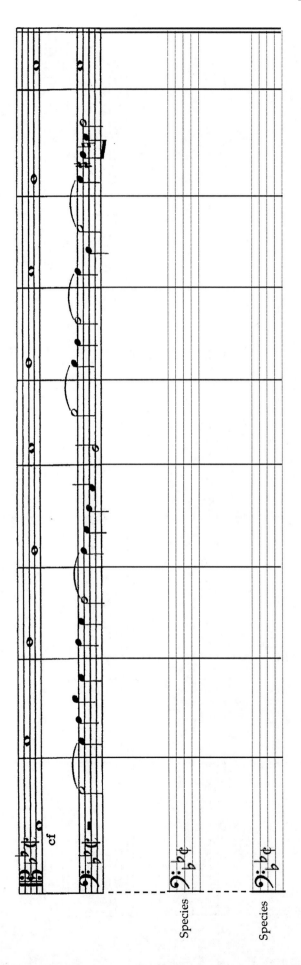

Species

Species

Fifth Species:

Counterpoint Assignment, no. 21

Name _____

Analyze the following excerpt, indicating each harmonic interval between the staves and identifying embellishing tones like Consonant Passing, (CP), Dissonant Passing (DP), Consonant Neighbors (CN), Dissonant Neighbors (DN), Double Neighbors (DN), *Nota Cambiatas* (NC), Suspensions (Sus), Syncopations (Syn), Decorate Resolutions (DR), etc. in the appropriate manner. Then compose two alternative counterpoints above the given *cantus firmus* that could represent simplifications of the given Fifth Species example, one in Second Species and one in First Species. Analyze the counterpoint between the *cantus firmus* and these counterpoints in the same way

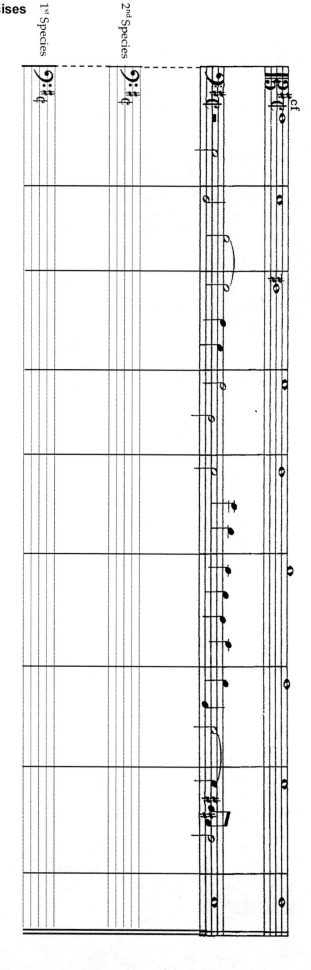

Fifth Species:

Counterpoint Assignment, no. 22

Name _____

Analyze the following excerpt, indicating each harmonic interval between the staves and identifying embellishing tones like Consonant Passing, (CP), Dissonant Passing (DP), Consonant Neighbors (CN), Dissonant Neighbors (DN), Double Neighbors (DN), *Nota Cambiatas* (NC), Suspensions (Sus), Syncopations (Syn), Decorate Resolutions (DR), etc. in the appropriate manner. Then compose two alternative counterpoints above the given *cantus firmus* that could represent simplifications of the given Fifth Species example, one in Fourth Species and one in First Species. Analyze the counterpoint between the *cantus firmus* and these counterpoints in the same way

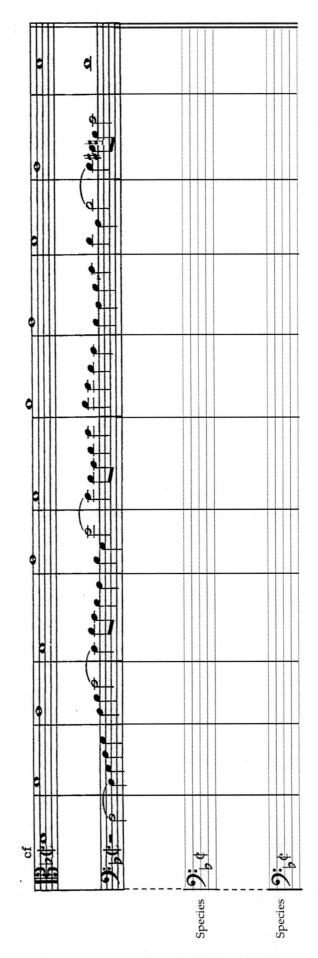